# Contents

# UNFRIEND THE ALGORITHM

## A Humorous Digital Detox Guide to Reclaiming Your Life

---

AVERY WELLS

# Introduction

Let me tell you about the day I realized my phone had not only eaten my breakfast but also swallowed my entire sense of self. It started innocently enough, as these things often do. I was scrolling through a social media feed when I noticed my toast had gone cold. Not that I had forgotten to eat it; I had simply spent forty-five minutes debating whether my cat could pull off a pirate costume for a photo. By the time I looked up, my herbal tea was lukewarm, and I had a new follower who was a bot selling discount sunglasses.

This book was born from that moment of clarity—or perhaps bewilderment—about how digital life can sneak up on us. My vision here is simple: to entertain you, educate you, and hopefully inspire a sigh of recognition as you think, "Ah, yes, I've been there too." We're on a journey to regain control of our digital lives, armed with a good dose of humor. After all, laughter is the best Wi-Fi password, or so I've heard.

Let's talk about the digital chaos we're all facing. With the constant ping of notifications and the pressure to project a perfect online persona, it's no wonder our mental health is feeling the strain.

Statistics show that the average person checks their phone 96 times a day. That's once every ten minutes! We live in a time when digital overload feels less like a gentle rain and more like a monsoon. And then there's social media, which can be a delightful playground one minute and a pressure cooker the next. We've got influencer culture convincing us that our morning smoothie isn't complete without a tropical backdrop, fake news making us question if we've slipped into an alternate reality, and clickbait that promises secrets to eternal youth but delivers endless pop-up ads instead.

Throughout this book, we'll explore these themes and more. From privacy concerns to the peculiar phenomenon of influencer culture, each chapter will unpack a different aspect of the social media landscape. And don't worry, we'll navigate these waters with humor as our compass. Imagine a world where we can laugh at the absurdity of it all while also arming ourselves with strategies to deal with it. For instance, consider the time I tried a digital detox and ended up having a very intense conversation with my toaster. I may have been a bit too committed to the idea of disconnecting, but at least the toaster listened.

Here's how the book is structured. Each chapter builds on the last, guiding you through a maze of digital habits and offering a comprehensive guide to managing your online life. We'll include interactive quizzes to test your social media savvy, real-life case studies showing how others cope, and reflection prompts to help you pause and think. By the end, you'll have a toolkit of strategies to keep the digital world from devouring your time and sanity.

Now, a bit about me. I'm someone who's passionate about helping you navigate this digital jungle. With years of experience studying the impact of technology on our lives, I've gathered insights and tips that I'm eager to share. My goal is to help you find balance, all while keeping things light-hearted and true to the quirks of modern life.

As we embark on this journey together, I encourage you to keep an open mind and a sense of humor. This book promises to be both entertaining and practical, offering a fresh perspective on how to survive and thrive in the social media trap. So, grab your favorite snack, silence your notifications, and let's get started on this adventure. Trust me, it'll be worth it—even if your toast gets cold.

ONE

# The Digital Overload Dilemma

Let me paint you a picture from my life—a scene that might feel all too familiar. There I was, enjoying a rare moment of solitude with a cup of java when suddenly my phone buzzed with a vengeance. A meme from a friend, "urgent" in its hilarity, demanded my immediate attention. Before I knew it, I was sucked into a vortex of group chat chaos, where the most pressing topic was whether pineapple belongs on pizza. An hour vanished, my java grew cold, and I was left wondering how a rectangle of glass had so much power over my day. It's this kind of digital distraction that has become the norm, a relentless barrage of notifications that keep us forever tethered to our devices, always on high alert for the next ping or buzz.

## Notifications: The Modern-Day Pavlov's Bell

If Pavlov were alive today, I'm convinced he'd swap his dogs for smartphones. The constant pinging of notifications conditions us much as those bells did to his canine companions, creating a world where our reactions are almost automatic. This cycle of alerts is more than just a minor irritation; it's a psychological experiment we're all unwittingly part of. We hear a buzz, feel a phantom vibration, and rush to our devices, only to find it was a figment of our imagination. This phenomenon, aptly named "Phantom Vibration Syndrome," is a testament to how deeply ingrained our response to these digital cues has become. Our brains have been rewired to expect that rush of dopamine, the same chemical that fuels our need for immediate gratification and keeps us checking our phones more often than we'd care to admit. Research indicates that some of us are bombarded by up to 200 notifications a day, each one a small assault on our attention span and emotional stability. These interruptions don't just fray our nerves; they can lead to increased anxiety and a time-warping sensation where hours slip by unnoticed.

But let's take a moment to laugh at ourselves. Have you ever found yourself in a meeting, trying to discreetly check your phone because of an "urgent" meme alert, only to realize it was a forwarded chain message from an enthusiastic relative? Or perhaps you've been stuck in a group chat avalanche where everyone insists on sharing their dessert photos, leaving your phone pinging incessantly. These scenarios are ripe for humor, yet they highlight a deeper issue: the triviality of many notifications compared to the urgency with which we treat them.

So, how do we combat this? Start by customizing your notification settings. Tailor them so that only the most important alerts break through your day. Many phones now offer a "Focus Mode," which can help sift through the noise, allowing you to concentrate on what truly matters. Consider scheduling specific times to check messages instead of succumbing to the constant lure of the next notification. This isn't just about saving time; it's about reclaiming control over your mental space.

Culturally, we've come to expect immediate responses to every message, a pressure cooker of social expectations that can lead to stress. In professional settings, the expectation to reply instantly can create a cycle of anxiety and distraction, reducing productivity and increasing burnout. It's important to recognize that while technology enables us to stay connected, it can also tether us to a continuous stream of demands.

## *Case Study: Conquering the Notification Overload*

Alex, a busy marketing manager, was drowning in notifications. Every few minutes, his phone would ping—texts, emails, social media updates, even reminders from an app tracking his water intake. The constant alerts made it hard for him to focus, and he felt more stressed than productive. One day, Alex realized it was time for a change after receiving a "Congrats on your steps!" notification from a fitness app in the middle of a client presentation. He took a step back and evaluated the notifications he truly needed, dividing them into three groups: "Must-See" for work emails and family messages, "Nice-to-Know" for app updates and news, and "Can-Wait" for everything else.

With this approach, Alex silenced all notifications that weren't essential, allowing only immediate work and family messages to appear during work hours. Over the next few days, he noticed a huge improvement in his concentration and mood. Instead of reacting to every ping, he could focus on his tasks and respond to updates when he had time. A month later, Alex checked in on his settings and even laughed at the "Nice-to-Know" group, including a long-forgotten cooking app congratulating him on imaginary achievements. By taking control of his notifications, Alex reduced his stress, increased his productivity, and reclaimed his time from the digital noise.

**Lesson**: Alex's experience highlights the power of customizing notifications to align with personal priorities. By categorizing alerts and adjusting settings, he could tame the "notification monster" and find greater focus and calm in his day.

***Interactive Exercise: Taming the Notification Monster***

Take a moment to assess your current notification settings. Reflect on the types of alerts you receive daily and categorize them into three groups: Must-See, Nice-to-Know, and Can-Wait. Adjust your settings to prioritize accordingly, and set a reminder to review this list monthly to ensure your digital life supports your real-world priorities.

By taking these steps, you can begin breaking the notification anxiety cycle. It's about finding a balance that allows you to enjoy the benefits of connectivity without falling prey to its pitfalls. And remember, humor can be your ally in this endeavor. Laugh at the absurdity of our digital dependencies and use that humor as a tool to navigate the complexities of the modern digital landscape.

## When Do Not Disturb is a Fantasy

There's a certain irony in modern technology's promise of peace wrapped up in those little crescent moon icons. The "Do Not Disturb" feature on our devices promises a sanctuary of silence, a refuge from digital chaos. Yet, in practice, it often feels like a well-meaning but unreliable bouncer at a party, letting in the very guests you hoped to avoid. Take, for instance, that crucial moment when you finally decide to meditate. You set your phone to "Do Not Disturb," settle into a zen-like state, and suddenly, your phone buzzes with the ferocity of a thousand bees. You open your eyes to find it is merely an alert about a new episode of a series you stopped watching seasons ago. Or worse, it's a "priority" call from your long-lost aunt who's excited to share her latest potato salad recipe. These interruptions, far from being rare, are all too common, blurring the lines of our attempts at digital detox.

The challenge of maintaining a "do not disturb" boundary is like managing a toddler in a candy store. It's a delicate balancing act, especially in a world where emergencies are subjective. We've all been there—setting our phones to silent mode, only to have it vibrate in the middle of a meeting because a friend decided their cat's new trick was an emergency worth sharing. The social guilt of not being available is another layer of complexity. It's as if we owe the world our constant presence, ready to respond at a moment's notice. It's not just about the fear of missing out; it's the anxiety of being perceived as absent or aloof.

Laughter often saves the day when technology fails us. There's something inherently comedic about the family group chat that bypasses all settings as if the phone has a "family override" function hardwired into its system. Or the friend who somehow knows precisely when you've had a long day and decides that's the perfect time to send a flurry of memes that demand immediate attention. These interruptions become stories we share and laugh about, yet they also highlight the need for more effective boundaries.

So, how do we make "Do Not Disturb" more than a polite suggestion to our phones? First, consider scheduling specific "do not disturb" hours. Choose times when you're least likely to miss anything critical and most in need of uninterrupted focus. This could be during work hours, family dinners, or even those precious moments before sleep. Communicate these boundaries to friends, family, and colleagues. Let them know when you're digitally unavailable and when you'll resurface. It's about setting expectations and reminding them that this isn't a snub but a necessity for your mental well-being.

## The Art of Selective Connectivity

In a world where the lines between work and personal life blur faster than a Snapchat story, mastering selective connectivity becomes not just a skill but a survival tactic. Picture this: you're at dinner with friends, trying to savor the moment, when your phone buzzes with a work email marked "urgent." You glance at it, then back at your friends, your mind now juggling between the present laughter and the looming tasks. This scenario is all too common yet entirely avoidable with a bit of digital discipline. Selective connectivity isn't about cutting yourself off from the world; it's about choosing when and how to engage. It's about prioritizing the people and moments that truly matter and granting yourself the grace to be fully present.

To begin this digital balancing act, start by identifying your VIP contacts. These are the folks whose calls you'd take even during a meteor shower—family, close friends, perhaps your boss (on occasion). Most smartphones allow you to create lists that give these select few priority access, ensuring their messages pierce through the noise without overwhelming you. This is digital triage at its finest, where you're not blocking the world out but letting the right parts of it in.

Now, let's talk about the mythical creature known as "Inbox Zero." Much like unicorns and calorie-free doughnuts, it's the stuff of legend—something we all strive for but rarely achieve. The idea of an empty inbox sounds like bliss, but the reality is often a game of digital whack-a-mole. Emails breed faster than rabbits, and just when you think you've cleared them all, another pops up with a cheery "just following up." Instead of chasing this elusive goal, focus on what's achievable: segregating your digital spaces. Keep work emails in one domain and personal ones in another. Use browser extensions or apps to fence off work-related content during personal time and vice versa. It's about creating compartments in your digital life to step into each with intention and clarity.

Selective connectivity also brings unexpected humor into our lives. Have you ever tried explaining to someone why you haven't responded to their text for two days? "Oh, sorry, you didn't make the VIP list" is a surefire way to get a laugh (or an awkward silence). But on a serious note, this approach allows for more meaningful interactions. By being more deliberate with your digital engagement, you reserve your attention for conversations that count, reducing the likelihood of miscommunications and digital faux pas.

Implementing selective connectivity doesn't require a major lifestyle overhaul. Start small by using apps that help manage your digital interactions. Tools like email filters, social media schedulers, and distraction blockers can guide your attention where needed most. These tools act like digital personal assistants, helping you navigate the constant influx of information without losing your mind. And remember, it's okay to have downtime. Just because you can be reached 24/7 doesn't mean you should be. Schedule regular breaks from your devices, allowing you to recharge without the digital hum in the background.

The benefits of stepping back from constant connectivity are manifold. For starters, it enhances your focus and productivity. When you're not perpetually tethered to your devices, you find more time to dive deep into tasks that require your full attention. Your brain thanks you, as does that project you've been putting off. Moreover, disconnecting from the digital world enhances real-world interactions. Conversations flow better when you're not constantly glancing at your phone, and you become more attuned to the subtleties of human interaction—the smile in your friend's eyes, the warmth in a shared joke. It's these moments that remind us of the richness of life outside the screen.

As we embrace selective connectivity, it's essential to remember that the goal isn't to isolate ourselves but to enrich our interactions. By choosing how we connect, we gain the freedom to be fully present in our lives, savoring the moments that matter most. Whether it's a quiet evening with a loved one or a productive afternoon at work, the power to choose is in your hands. So, let's take a moment to breathe, step back, and embrace the beauty of a life well-connected but not over-connected.

TWO

# The Privacy Paradox

I found myself in a predicament the other day, which, as these things often go, began with an innocent impulse to share. I posted a picture of my breakfast—an artful arrangement of avocado toast and a perfectly brewed cappuccino—and declared it "Brunch goals!" Little did I know that my gleeful caption would open the floodgates to a cascade of comments, ranging from genuine admiration to unsolicited advice on avocado oxidation and conspiracy theories about caffeine's impact on the economy. It became apparent that my innocent post had spiraled into a public spectacle, all because I decided to broadcast my morning meal to the world.

## Sharing is Scaring: The Oversharing Epidemic

In today's digital landscape, the art of oversharing has become an accidental hobby for many. Social media encourages us to life-cast every moment, transforming our existence into a continuous stream of updates. From posting selfies with our pets to sharing our late-night musings about existential dread, the urge to document and share is relentless. The pressure to maintain an online presence often feels like a never-ending audition for a reality show, where the judges are an audience of acquaintances and strangers alike. This phenomenon is not just amusing but can be profoundly revealing. Why do we feel compelled to share every meal, every mood swing, every mundane detail of our existence? According to a 2022 study, college students often view excessive posting about personal issues as oversharing, suggesting that even the younger, digital-native generation recognizes the fine line between sharing and overexposure.

The humor in oversharing is undeniable. Who hasn't cringed after posting a vague status that spiraled into a misunderstanding? I once cryptically posted, "Can't believe this happened today!" and left it at that. I was merely lamenting a parking ticket, but by the end of the day, my comments section was rife with theories ranging from a breakup to an alien abduction. The pitfalls of sharing too much can lead to unexpected embarrassment. It's like when a friend posted about their "secret" engagement party, only to have it spoiled by an overzealous guest tagging them in every photo. Such tales are humorous in hindsight but serve as cautionary tales about the risks of excessive disclosure.

On a more serious note, oversharing can have significant consequences. Identity theft is a real threat, often exacerbated by the personal details we unwittingly share online. When we disclose information about our daily routines, vacation plans, or even our full names and birthdays, we provide potential identity thieves with all the ammunition they need. Additionally, unwanted attention and privacy invasion are lurking risks. Sharing your real-time location through check-ins or tagging can inadvertently invite strangers into your life, crossing boundaries you didn't even know you had. The "privacy calculus effect" suggests we constantly weigh the benefits of social validation against the potential privacy risks, yet this calculation often errs on the side of oversharing.

In navigating this digital conundrum, smart sharing becomes paramount. Consider limiting the personal details available on your public profiles. Do you really need the entire internet to know your favorite color or your grandmother's maiden name? Privacy settings are your best friends here. They allow you to control who sees what, ensuring your content is visible only to those you trust. Thoughtful posting and content curation can transform your digital footprint from a sprawling mess into a curated gallery that reflects who you are without giving away too much. Before you post, pause and ask yourself: Is this something I'd be comfortable discussing in a crowded room? If not, it might be wise to keep it offline.

Lastly, laugh at the absurdity of our digital tendencies. Embrace the humor in those oversharing moments, and let them serve as gentle reminders of our shared humanity in this hyper-connected world. If nothing else, they make for great stories at dinner parties. And remember, while it's natural to want to share your life, it's equally important to protect the parts that are just for you. So, go ahead and post that picture of your brunch, but maybe keep the existential musings to yourself—or at least save them for the next chapter of your memoir.

### *Case Study: The Oversharing Spiral*

Lily, a young professional and avid social media user, loved sharing snapshots of her daily life—from her morning coffee to weekend adventures. One day, she posted a picture of her new apartment's view with the caption, "Finally moved in!" Unknowingly, the photo included enough visual landmarks for anyone familiar with the area to pinpoint her location. Within hours, she received comments and messages from acquaintances asking if she lived in a specific building. Feeling a twinge of concern, she realized how vulnerable she'd made herself by casually sharing her surroundings online.

Disturbed by the experience, Lily started reflecting on the details she was freely giving away. She began limiting the personal information in her posts, double-checking her privacy settings, and sharing only with close friends. She also became more mindful of her "digital footprint," recognizing that oversharing can lead to unintended exposure. By dialing back the public aspect of her online life, Lily enjoyed the benefits of sharing while protecting her privacy. This experience reminded her of the balance between openness and caution in a hyper-connected world.

**Lesson**: Lily's story underscores the importance of thoughtful sharing in an age of digital transparency. By carefully managing what she shares and who sees it, she took control of her privacy, demonstrating that digital boundaries are essential for personal security.

### *Interactive Exercise: Crafting Your Digital Boundaries*

Take a moment to reflect on your own sharing habits. Consider your recent posts—did they contain more personal information than necessary? List a few adjustments you can make to strengthen your digital boundaries, such as limiting location tags or refining your privacy settings. Recognize that privacy isn't about cutting yourself off from the online world but about making mindful choices that protect your sense of security. Remember, the details you hold back can be just as powerful as the ones you choose to share.

## The Privacy Pirouette: Dancing with Data Theft

Imagine waking up one morning to find that your bank account has been emptied. Not because you splurged on a spontaneous trip to Hawaii but because someone, somewhere, decided your identity was up for grabs. This unsettling scenario is a reality for many, a consequence of data theft that lurks in the shadows of our digital interactions. Data theft occurs when unauthorized individuals gain access to personal information. It often begins with phishing attacks, those pesky emails pretending to be your bank or favorite online store, urging you to click a link because "your account needs immediate attention." Falling for these can lead you down a rabbit hole where your sensitive information is harvested before you finish your morning coffee. Then there are the more sophisticated social engineering tactics, where cybercriminals manipulate you into divulging details by masquerading as trusted entities. And let's not forget about data breaches, those large-scale leaks where your personal data is exposed to the world due to lax security measures. It's a digital minefield out there.

Security mishaps can be downright comical if they weren't so concerning. Take, for instance, the classic blunder of setting "password" as your password. It's the digital equivalent of leaving your front door wide open with a welcome sign. Or when an overly eager colleague fell for an obviously fake phishing email, complete with typos that would make your third-grade teacher cringe. You know the ones—"Click here to claim your $1,000,000 prize!" Yet, in a moment of distraction, it's easy to click without thinking. These blunders, while humorous in hindsight, highlight a broader issue: our casual approach to data security. It's a bit like walking through a haunted house with a blindfold, assuming nothing will jump out because it hasn't yet.

So, how do you protect yourself against these digital gremlins? First, embrace the mantra of strong, unique passwords. Yes, they're a hassle to remember, but they're your first line of defense. Consider a password manager to help keep track of them all without resorting to sticky notes on your monitor. Next, enable two-factor authentication wherever possible. This adds an extra layer of security, like a moat around your digital castle. Even if someone cracks your password, they'll need a second piece of information to get through. Be cautious about sharing personal data on unsecured networks as well. Public Wi-Fi is convenient, but it's also an open invitation for data thieves to swoop in and snatch your information. Instead, use a virtual private network (VPN) to encrypt your connection and keep prying eyes at bay.

The balance between convenience and security is a delicate dance. Let's face it, easy-to-remember passwords are tempting. Who wants to juggle a series of random letters, numbers, and symbols when "123456" is so simple? But simplicity often comes at a cost, leaving you vulnerable to cyber threats. Security measures, while sometimes cumbersome, are like locking your doors at night. They may slow you down, but they're crucial for peace of mind. The impact of these precautions on user experience is undeniable. It's a bit like adding a seatbelt to a roller coaster—necessary but slightly inconvenient. Yet, these small sacrifices in convenience are worthwhile when considering the alternative: the chaos of dealing with a breach.

As you navigate your digital life, remember that a little vigilance goes a long way. Treat your personal information with the same care you'd give to your most prized possessions. After all, in the digital age, your data is worth its weight in gold. Be proactive, stay informed, and don't let the specter of data theft catch you off guard. Keep your digital footprint secure, and with any luck, you'll avoid the pitfalls that have caught so many others unaware.

## Incognito Mode: The Illusion of Anonymity

There's a common misconception that incognito mode is the digital equivalent of an invisibility cloak, allowing you to roam the internet without leaving a trace. But if you've ever tried using it to stealthily shop for surprise gifts or indulge in some late-night guilty pleasures, you'd know it's more like wearing a flamboyant disguise—you're still there, just slightly harder to recognize. Despite popular belief, incognito mode doesn't make you anonymous online. It merely stops your browser from saving your history, cookies, and site data. Your internet service provider, employer, or even the websites you visit can still track your activity. It's like cleaning up your room by shoving everything under the bed; the mess may be hidden from casual observation, but it's far from gone.

The belief in incognito mode's magical powers leads to some hilarious overestimations of privacy. People often assume it's a digital force field, leading to overconfident behaviors. I once heard about someone who used incognito mode to plan a surprise party on a shared family computer, only to discover their browsing history wasn't the only thing they needed to hide. The surprise was spoiled not by snooping siblings but by an email confirmation sent to the family's joint account. The false sense of security provided by incognito mode can embolden us to act recklessly online, believing we're shielded from prying eyes when, in fact, we're still quite exposed.

Digital footprints are like breadcrumbs we drop every time we venture into the online world. Websites plant cookies and tracking scripts that follow us, learning our habits and preferences. It's a bit like leaving a trail of glitter—nearly impossible to clean up completely. Your IP address also acts as a digital fingerprint, revealing your location and potentially your identity. Even metadata, the data about data, can reveal patterns about your online behavior, painting a picture of who you are based on where you've been. This persistent trail is why advertisers seem to know you better than your closest friends, bombarding you with eerily relevant ads moments after you've casually mentioned needing new running shoes.

So, how do you enhance your online privacy beyond the false comfort of incognito mode? Start by incorporating a virtual private network, or VPN, into your browsing routine. A VPN masks your IP address, making your online activity harder to trace back to you. It's like donning a different disguise whenever you enter the digital realm. Clearing cookies and browsing history regularly is another simple yet effective step to reduce your digital footprint. Consider it a regular housecleaning, sweeping away the bits of data left behind.

Also, be mindful of app permissions and data sharing, as many apps request access to far more information than they need to function. It's worth taking a moment to review these settings and adjust them to protect your privacy.

In our quest for privacy, it's important to balance caution with practicality. We live in a connected world where sharing some information is inevitable. Yet, by being mindful of our digital habits, we can navigate this landscape with greater awareness and security. As we wrap up this chapter on privacy, remember that anonymity online is more myth than reality. With a bit of humor and a few practical steps, you can manage your digital presence without falling into the trap of false security. Now, let's move forward, knowing that while the digital world is full of challenges, it's also brimming with opportunities to connect and thrive.

THREE

# Social Media Showdown

Picture this: it's a Saturday night, and you're cozy in bed, ready for a restful sleep. But then, a notification pops up—a friend's beach party, complete with palm trees, laughter, and a suspiciously perfect sunset. Suddenly, your evening feels inadequate, and there you are, wide awake, scrolling through everyone else's highlight reel. Welcome to the world of Fear of Missing Out, or FOMO, where social media serves as both the stage and the audience for our curated lives. FOMO isn't just about missing events; it's about the perception that everyone else is living their best life while you're stuck at home with your cat and a cup of lukewarm tea. It's a fear deeply rooted in the human psyche, a modern twist on the age-old anxiety of being left out of the tribe.

On platforms like Instagram, FOMO thrives on what I affectionately call the "Highlight Reel" syndrome. You're bombarded with images of perfect vacations, exquisite meals, and seemingly flawless relationships. It's as if everyone else lives in perpetual daylight while your life is stuck in a loop of mundane Mondays. But here's the catch: these highlight reels are just that—highlights. They don't capture the late-night existential crises or the mornings when you spill coffee on your shirt. The illusion of perfect lives is powerful, but it's just that—an illusion. In reality, everyone is sifting through the same pile of daily chaos, just like you.

Let's take a lighthearted look at how FOMO drives us to irrational behaviors. Have you ever found yourself at an event you have no interest in, just so you can post a quick snap to prove you have a life? Maybe you've stayed up until midnight, frantically checking friends' stories, fearful that you'll miss that one crucial moment that will never actually matter. It's like being a digital Cinderella, afraid that the social media clock will strike twelve, and you'll turn back into a pumpkin of irrelevance. These behaviors are more common than you think and are often met with equal parts humor and exasperation.

Breaking free from the FOMO cycle requires more than just putting your phone on airplane mode. It involves a shift in perspective and a conscious effort to practice gratitude and mindfulness. Start by setting specific times for social media usage, much like you would schedule a meeting or a meal. This simple act can significantly reduce anxiety and help you focus on the present moment. Curate your feed by following accounts that promote positivity and realism. Seek out influencers who share both their triumphs and their trials, giving you a more balanced view of life.

Another powerful tool in combating FOMO is the social media detox. Imagine taking a break from the digital world, even if just for a weekend. The benefits are profound: a chance to reset perspectives, reduce stress, and reconnect with the tangible world around you. Personal stories of digital detoxes often reveal unexpected joys—a newfound appreciation for nature, an engaging conversation without the interruption of notifications, or even discovering the simple pleasure of reading a book uninterrupted. According to a recent study, participants who limited their social media use to 30 minutes per day experienced significant improvements in life satisfaction and reduced stress levels.

### *Case Study: A Week of Digital Detox*

A college senior, Maya often lost hours each evening to social media. What started as a quick check-in to see her friends' posts became hours of scrolling through highlight reels, travel photos, and viral videos. Realizing her sleep and focus were suffering, she tried a "digital detox" experiment, starting with just three hours of screen-free time each day. She used these hours to explore hobbies she'd set aside, like painting and journaling. By the end of the week, Maya noticed she was more energized and focused during her study sessions, and she had reconnected with activities that felt truly fulfilling.

Encouraged by her progress, Maya extended her digital detox to full weekends, dedicating them to in-person experiences rather than online updates. She also started journaling about her feelings, tracking the positive shifts in her mood and social interactions. She didn't miss the constant updates but appreciated her newfound time and focus. This small detox experiment allowed Maya to step back from the "highlight reel" and reconnect with her life meaningfully, reminding her that joy and fulfillment exist outside the screen.

**Lesson**: Maya's story shows that even small breaks from social media can significantly improve mood, focus, and personal fulfillment. By dedicating time away from screens, she discovered the value of being present and found contentment in the simple moments.

### *Interactive Exercise: Your Digital Detox Plan*

Consider trying a digital detox of your own. Start small—perhaps just a few hours each day—gradually building up to longer periods. Journal your experiences. Note any changes in mood, focus, or social interactions. Reflect on what you miss and what you're relieved to leave behind. This exercise can provide valuable insights into your relationship with social media and help you regain control.

Ultimately, navigating the social media landscape requires a blend of awareness, humor, and practical strategies. By recognizing the illusion of the highlight reel, embracing mindfulness, and exploring the benefits of a digital detox, you can interrupt the FOMO feedback loop and find contentment in the here and now. So, the next time you find yourself on the brink of a midnight scrolling spree, remember that the most important moments are happening right where you are, with or without a hashtag.

## Ghosting and the Ghosted: A Comedy of Errors

Ghosting, the modern-day Houdini act of vanishing without a trace, has become a staple in the digital age. It's the social media equivalent of slipping out of a party without saying goodbye, except the party is a perpetual chat thread, and your sudden absence is noticed by everyone except, perhaps, the host. The roots of ghosting lie in the ease and anonymity digital interactions afford us. It's remarkably simple to disappear when all it takes is a few taps on the screen to block, unfriend, or mute someone from our lives. No awkward face-to-face confrontations, no drawn-out explanations—just a clean, albeit abrupt, break. This disappearing act often occurs in casual dating scenarios, where the stakes feel lower and the perceived obligation to communicate diminishes. But it can also happen in friendships, professional relationships, and even family interactions, leaving the ghosted party to wonder what went wrong.

The awkwardness that follows ghosting can be unintentionally hilarious. Imagine scrolling through social media one lazy afternoon, mindlessly liking posts, when you accidentally double-tap a photo of someone you ghosted months ago. Your heart skips a beat as you realize you've just resurfaced in their notifications, like a ghost who forgot they were supposed to be invisible. Or consider the ghosters who reappear out of the blue, suddenly texting as if their prolonged absence was just a minor blip in the timeline. "Hey, what's up?" they casually type, as if they haven't been MIA for half a year. These moments highlight the absurdity and misunderstandings inherent in ghosting—where the digital dance of disappearing and reappearing leaves us bewildered and bemused.

For those on the receiving end of ghosting, the emotional fallout can be surprisingly impactful. It's like watching a magic trick without the prestige; you're left in the lurch, wondering how and why someone could vanish so completely. But rather than wallowing in rejection, why not create a "ghosted" playlist? Fill it with cathartic tunes—think Adele-level heartbreak mixed with empowering anthems. Let the music remind you that while one connection may have fizzled, your playlist is still going strong. There's humor in rejection, too. After all, what's more quintessentially human than experiencing—and laughing at—life's little letdowns?

Direct communication could mitigate much of the ghosting epidemic. Imagine a world where people craft tactful yet honest messages to express disinterest. Instead of fading into digital oblivion, they might send a simple, "Hey, I enjoyed our chats, but I don't see this going further." Sure, it's a bit uncomfortable, but it also clears the fog of uncertainty. Addressing issues head-on has its perks. It fosters emotional intelligence, builds resilience, and, most importantly, treats others with the respect they deserve. When you give someone closure, you also gift them the ability to move on with clarity and dignity.

In an era where communication is dominated by screens, ghosting remains a peculiar paradox. It's both a product of convenience and a source of discomfort. But by embracing humor, practicing empathy, and advocating for honest dialogue, we can navigate this digital landscape gracefully—or at least with fewer awkward encounters. So, next time you feel the urge to pull a ghosting stunt, consider the comedy of errors it might unleash. You might just find that a little honesty goes a long way, leaving behind a trail of laughter instead of confusion.

## Viral Validation: Chasing the Like-Button High

In the digital age, the pursuit of likes has become a cultural phenomenon, often dictating how we present ourselves online. It's that tiny heart or thumbs-up that can make or break our day, a symbol of approval that sends dopamine rushing through our brains every time our phone buzzes with a new notification. This isn't just a fleeting feeling; it's a scientifically backed response where our brain's reward system lights up like a Christmas tree, making us crave more. Social media platforms have mastered this art of validation, turning us into eager participants in a game where metrics and analytics rule supreme. We obsess over numbers, tracking the rise and fall of our followers, engagements, and shares as if each statistic were a direct reflection of our worth. It's an addiction that feeds on itself, leaving us hungry for more with every double-tap and retweet.

The lengths people go to in their quest for validation can be both impressive and absurd. Take, for instance, the elaborate photoshoots orchestrated for what should be a simple post. A friend of mine once spent an entire afternoon arranging flowers, adjusting lighting, and capturing the perfect shot of her morning coffee, only to caption it "Just a casual morning." The irony was not lost on her—nor on the rest of us, who chuckled at the amount of effort behind the supposed spontaneity. Then there are the dramatic reactions to minimal engagement, where a post that receives fewer likes than expected becomes a minor existential crisis. You might find yourself refreshing the page obsessively, questioning your social media strategy, or worse, considering deleting the offending post altogether, convinced it's somehow tarnished your online persona.

But what if there's a better way to seek validation beyond the metrics? Focusing on real-life achievements and relationships can provide a more enduring sense of accomplishment. Consider celebrating personal milestones privately; not everything needs to be broadcast to the world. Relish in the joy of achieving a personal goal or receiving heartfelt praise from someone who genuinely cares rather than the fleeting satisfaction of digital applause. This shift in focus can help break the cycle of dependency on likes and shares, allowing you to find fulfillment in experiences that can't be quantified.

Redefining success in today's digital landscape is a crucial step toward achieving a healthier relationship with social media. It starts by emphasizing quality over quantity in our online and offline interactions. Genuine connections hold more value than a large follower count, and meaningful conversations trump the number of comments on a post. Promoting content that aligns with personal values can also lead to a more authentic online presence. When you create and share content that truly resonates with your beliefs and passions, the validation you receive becomes a welcome side effect rather than the primary goal.

Pursuing likes and validation can often feel like chasing an ever-elusive high, but it doesn't have to be this way. By shifting our focus to real-world connections and redefining what success looks like in our digital age, we can begin to break free from the cycle of seeking approval through screens. As we explore these changes, remember that humor and self-awareness are powerful tools in this process. Laugh at the absurdity of staging a photoshoot for your breakfast, celebrate the moments that matter outside the digital realm, and embrace the freedom that comes with prioritizing authenticity over appearance.

As we conclude our exploration of the social media showdown, we've examined the intricate dance between connection and disconnection in the digital world. From the pervasive fear of missing out to the pursuit of viral validation, each aspect of our online lives presents both challenges and opportunities for growth. The next chapter will delve into the influencer illusion, examining how curated personas shape our perceptions and exploring strategies to navigate this ever-evolving landscape with clarity and confidence.

# FOUR

# The Influencer Illusion

Once upon a time, influencers were simply the friends who convinced you to switch your choice of shampoo or try that weird sushi place around the corner. Fast forward to today, and these digital demigods have transformed into orchestrators of perfectly curated online worlds, where every selfie is a snapshot of "effortless" perfection. But let's not kid ourselves—behind each immaculate photo lies a tale of countless retakes, strategic angles, and the occasional meltdown over bad lighting. It's a world where the hashtag hustle meets the art of illusion, and we, the audience, are often left wondering how they make it look so easy.

In the age of social media, the influencer image is meticulously crafted through techniques that would make a professional marketing team proud. Staged lifestyle photoshoots are the bread and butter of an influencer's feed, often involving a small army of props, outfits, and, let's be honest, a bit of chaos. Picture this: an influencer sprawled on a picnic blanket, surrounded by a picturesque spread of food that's more art than lunch. What you don't see is the assistant frantically swatting away bugs or the influencer themselves precariously balancing on one elbow to avoid squishing the sandwiches. The final image? A serene afternoon in the park. The reality? A comedy of errors that would make for a far more entertaining post.

Of course, the overuse of filters and photo editing apps can't be ignored. With a few swipes and taps, skin becomes flawless, eyes sparkle with unnatural clarity, and even the sky turns a more vibrant shade of blue. These digital enhancements create a reality that's ironically more fictional than any fairy tale. The strategic deployment of hashtags further amplifies this idealized image, reaching wider audiences and ensuring that even your grandma's neighbor's dog has seen the post by lunchtime. Yet, as we scroll through these images, it's easy to forget the countless hours of editing behind them.

The comedic contrast between these polished images and real life is brilliantly captured by the "Instagram vs. Reality" meme trend. These memes juxtapose the glamorous with the genuine, revealing the hilarity that ensues when expectations meet reality. Behind-the-scenes blunders during content creation often tell a far more relatable story. Think of the influencer trying to capture a candid laugh, only to trip over their own feet, or the makeup tutorial gone awry when the eyeliner transforms into something resembling a toddler's attempt at finger painting.

These curated images can significantly impact followers' self-esteem and perceptions of reality, often perpetuating the illusion of effortless success. The pressure to emulate influencer lifestyles can weigh heavily on viewers, leading to feelings of inadequacy and envy. A study highlighted in Bored Panda suggests that these idealized portrayals contribute to higher risks of depression, anxiety, and low self-esteem, particularly among young women. The constant comparison to these manufactured realities can make followers feel like they're falling short despite knowing on some level that what they're seeing is far from genuine.

But there's hope in promoting authenticity amidst all the smoke and mirrors. Engaging with creators who share unfiltered content can be a refreshing change, offering a more genuine glimpse into their lives. Celebrate individuality and imperfections by following those who aren't afraid to show the occasional blemish or embrace a messy room in the background. It's these moments of honesty that remind us that life isn't always picture-perfect—and that's perfectly okay.

### *Case Study: Choosing Authenticity Over Perfection*

Emma, a graphic designer with a small but loyal Instagram following, had always been captivated by influencers who seemed to live flawlessly curated lives. She followed accounts that showcased picture-perfect homes, designer clothes, and glamorous vacations. Over time, though, Emma felt discouraged, as if her own life didn't measure up. She realized that the influencers she followed fueled an endless pursuit of perfection, leaving her feeling more drained than inspired.

Determined to shift her mindset, Emma searched for creators who celebrated authenticity and showed life's messy, imperfect parts. She also committed to bringing more realness to her feed, sharing candid moments and behind-the-scenes snapshots of her design process, including the "trial-and-error" messes and creative blocks. Her followers responded positively to her surprise, with many expressing relief at seeing a more relatable side of her life. This journey helped Emma appreciate her path and reminded her that she didn't need a flawless online persona to connect meaningfully with others.

**Lesson**: Emma's experience shows the value of curating a social media environment that promotes authenticity. Following accounts that reflect genuine values and sharing her unfiltered moments, she found a more fulfilling and self-affirming approach to social media.

### *Interactive Exercise: Celebrating the Real You*

Consider taking a moment to reflect on the influencers you follow. Are they promoting authenticity, or are they feeding into the illusion of perfection? Challenge yourself to seek out voices that align with your values and celebrate the beauty of imperfection. Jot down a few thoughts on how you can embrace authenticity in your own social media presence, whether it's by sharing a candid moment or showing a behind-the-scenes glimpse of your own daily life.

As we continue to navigate the world of influencers and their digital illusions, remember that the power of social media lies not just in what we consume but in how we choose to engage with it. By appreciating authenticity over perfection, we reclaim our sense of self and find joy in the beautifully imperfect tapestry of our lives.

## The Sponsored Life: Product Placement in Personal Branding

Imagine scrolling through your feed only to discover your favorite influencer, who normally shares travel tips or personal stories, suddenly pivoting to extol the virtues of a new brand of protein powder. It feels a bit like watching a dramatic plot twist in a sitcom—unexpected and a tad out of place. This is the world of sponsored content, where product placement is as ubiquitous as those perfectly filtered selfies. In the wild terrain of social media, influencers sprinkle their content with endorsements, sometimes subtly, other times with the finesse of a sledgehammer.

The prevalence of product placement in influencer content is no accident. It's a carefully orchestrated dance between brands and influencers, designed to catch your attention and, hopefully, convince you to part with your hard-earned cash. While there are regulations in place to ensure transparency—think hashtags like #ad or #sponsored—it's often a fine line between genuine endorsement and paid promotion. Influencers are tasked with the delicate job of weaving sponsored content seamlessly into their brand, like trying to pass off a store-bought pie as homemade at

Thanksgiving dinner. When done well, it can feel like a natural extension of their persona. When done poorly, it's as jarring as a cat in a dog show.

Now, let's have a giggle at some of the more absurd moments in influencer endorsements. Picture a fitness influencer known for their minimalist lifestyle suddenly promoting a luxury handbag brand. Or a vegan blogger singing the praises of a new steakhouse. It's these over-the-top product placements that often leave us scratching our heads, wondering if we missed a memo or if the influencer simply needed to pay this month's rent. There's a humorous absurdity in watching influencers try to sell products that seemingly clash with their established image, like trying to fit a square peg into a round hole.

Trust is the currency of the influencer world, and maintaining it while engaging in sponsored collaborations requires a deft touch. Clearly labeling sponsored posts is crucial. It's like wearing a name tag at a networking event—it lets everyone know exactly who you are and what you're about. Sharing honest reviews and personal experiences with products can further cement credibility, allowing followers to see that the influencer's endorsement isn't just a cash grab but a genuine affinity for the product. Balancing sponsored content with personal stories is another way influencers can maintain authenticity. They can create an engaging and believable narrative by weaving in relatable anecdotes or personal insights.

As a consumer in this digital marketplace, becoming more discerning is key to ensuring you're not swept away by the tide of influencer marketing. Start by researching products before making a purchase. A quick search can reveal a wealth of information, from customer reviews to ingredient lists. Recognizing the marketing tactics employed by influencers can also arm you with the knowledge needed to make informed decisions. Is the post saturated with buzzwords like "life-changing" or "must-have"? Are the comments filled with similar endorsements from other influencers? These can be telltale signs of a coordinated marketing campaign.

Approaching influencer content with a critical eye doesn't mean you need to become a cynic but rather a savvy consumer. By understanding the mechanics behind the sponsored life, you can enjoy the creativity and inspiration influencers offer without falling prey to every product they promote. So the next time you see an influencer touting the latest and greatest gadget, take a moment to pause, chuckle at the spectacle, and decide if it truly fits into your life —or if it's just another piece of the sponsored puzzle.

## Influenced by Influencers: Finding Real Inspiration

In the sprawling landscape of social media, amidst the carefully curated selfies and product endorsements, lies a glimmer of genuine influence that has the potential to spark positive change. Imagine scrolling through your feed and stumbling upon an influencer not selling a brand but advocating for a cause. These influencers champion social causes, using their platforms to raise awareness on issues like climate change, education, and mental health. Their posts aren't mere cries for attention but rather calls to action, inviting followers to join them in making a difference. Their stories often include personal experiences, highlighting struggles with mental health or the triumphs of overcoming adversity. This transparency and vulnerability can inspire followers to reflect on their own lives and perhaps even take steps towards change.

The power of influence extends beyond calls to action. It also lies in the imitation it inspires. They say imitation is the sincerest form of flattery, but it's also a source of humor. Cue the "copycat" phenomenon, where followers mimic influencer fashion choices, hairstyles, or even morning routines, hoping to capture a slice of that seemingly effortless lifestyle. The results can be as endearing as they are entertaining. Picture a devoted fan trying to recreate a complex yoga pose posted by their favorite wellness influencer, only to end up in a tangled heap on the living room floor. Or the culinary enthusiast who, inspired by a food blogger, attempts an intricate soufflé, only to produce something more like scrambled eggs. These moments of imitation bring a sense of connection and community, even if they don't always hit the mark.

But how do you sift through the noise to find influencers who offer meaningful and inspiring content? It begins with seeking out niche influencers who have genuine passions. Perhaps there's a creator who shares your love for vintage vinyl records or another who documents their journey in sustainable living. These niche influencers may not have millions of followers, but their content resonates deeply with their audience. Engaging with creators who prioritize community over popularity is key. These influencers are less concerned with follower counts and more focused on fostering connections and sharing knowledge. Their authenticity shines through, making their content not just something to consume but something to experience.

While influencers can inspire, it's important to remember that you, too, have the power to influence. Creating personal influence begins with developing a personal brand based on your core values. What do you stand for? What stories do you want to share? Whether you're passionate about photography, cooking, or social justice, sharing personal insights and experiences with others can create ripples of influence in your own circles. It's not about going viral or gaining followers but about connecting with others in meaningful ways. Your experiences, struggles, and triumphs have the power to inspire those around you, whether through a heartfelt conversation, a blog post, or a simple social media update.

In a world where the line between genuine and contrived influence often blurs, finding real inspiration requires intentionality. By seeking out influencers who advocate for positive change, embracing humor in our imitations, and nurturing our own capacity for influence, we can navigate this digital landscape with clarity and purpose. As we wrap up this chapter, consider how you can engage with the digital world in a way that fosters growth, connection, and authenticity. Remember, the most valuable influence is not about changing others but inspiring them to discover the best versions of themselves. Now, as we continue exploring the complexities of digital life, let's see what the next chapter holds in store.

# FIVE

# Navigating News and Clickbait

I was enjoying the calming ritual of jasmine tea when I stumbled upon a headline that promised to reveal "The Secret to Eternal Youth." Intrigued—and admittedly a little hopeful—I clicked, only to find myself knee-deep in an article about the benefits of drinking more water. There I was, a willing victim of clickbait, lured by the promise of everlasting vitality and left with the age-old advice of staying hydrated. It was a stark reminder that in the world of online content, not everything is as it seems. Clickbait is a master of disguise, using sensationalism to grab our attention and lead us down a path of exaggerated claims and emotional manipulation. Those "You Won't Believe What Happens Next" headlines are the digital equivalent of candy-coated promises, preying on our innate curiosity and desire for surprise.

Understanding how clickbait works is like unmasking a magician's trick. It thrives on emotionally charged language, crafting headlines that provoke curiosity or stir up intense emotions such as anger or excitement. A study published by Wired explains that this emotional arousal is a key ingredient, as it triggers engagement by exploiting our natural instincts. The promise of a shocking twist or revelation is often too tantalizing to resist, pulling us in with the allure of the unknown. However, like most magic tricks, the reality is often less impressive than the buildup. Many times, these hyperbolic claims lead to mundane stories that barely deliver on their promises, leaving us with a sense of anticlimax.

The humor in these deceptive headlines is almost as entertaining as the articles themselves. We've all encountered those ridiculous claims that promise to "Change Your Life Forever" or reveal "The One Thing Doctors Don't Want You to Know." Yet, more often than not, the life-changing secret is something as anticlimactic as "eat more vegetables." Misleading thumbnails add to the comedy with eye-catching images that often promise more than they deliver. It's like being enticed by a movie poster featuring an epic space battle, only to find that the film is a slow documentary about potato farming. These exaggerations might make us chuckle and erode our trust in digital media.

The impact of clickbait on reader trust is significant. An IEEE Transactions on Technology and Society study found that clickbait headlines significantly reduce the credibility of news items. When headlines repeatedly fail to deliver, readers feel misled and frustrated, which can lead to a broader skepticism towards online content. The spread of misinformation through viral clickbait articles only compounds this issue, as sensationalized stories often gain traction before their inaccuracies can be debunked. This erosion of trust creates a vicious cycle, where genuine news struggles to stand out amidst the noise of exaggerated headlines.

### Case Study: Breaking Free from the Clickbait Trap

Raj, a busy office manager, often found himself sucked into clickbait headlines during his lunch breaks. Headlines like "You Won't Believe What Happened Next" or "Shocking Secrets of Your Favorite Celebrities" constantly grabbed his attention. However, each time he clicked, he felt disappointed; the articles rarely delivered on their promises, and he'd lose valuable time that could have been spent relaxing. Realizing how much these attention-grabbing headlines cost him, Raj decided to examine his clickbait habits and find ways to spot sensationalized content before falling for it.

Raj began by identifying common clickbait patterns, noting that certain words and phrases were designed to spark curiosity but often led to shallow or misleading content. He made a mental list of red-flag phrases, like "You'll Never Guess" and "The Shocking Truth." Instead of clicking immediately, he takes a moment to consider the source. He skips it if it's from an unfamiliar site with a reputation for exaggeration. Over time, Raj found that he consumed more quality content and felt less frustrated by empty headlines. This small shift helped him reclaim his break time and cultivate a more discerning approach to online content.

**Lesson**: Raj's experience highlights the value of developing a skeptical eye when approaching sensationalized headlines. By recognizing clickbait patterns and focusing on reputable sources, he was able to break the cycle of disappointment and use his time more mindfully.

### *Interactive Exercise: Spotting Clickbait*

Let's take a moment to reflect on our own clickbait encounters. Think about the last few headlines that caught your eye—were they overly sensationalized? Did they deliver on their promises or leave you feeling short-changed? Use this reflection to help hone your skills in identifying clickbait and make a mental note of common phrases and patterns that tend to lure you in.

Resisting the siren call of clickbait requires a keen eye and a healthy dose of skepticism. Start by identifying common clickbait phrases and patterns. Phrases like "You Won't Believe" or "Shocking Truth" are often red flags. Before clicking, take a moment to verify the credibility of the source. Is it a reputable news outlet or an obscure site with a dubious reputation? These small steps can help you navigate the digital landscape with greater discernment and avoid falling into the trap of sensationalized content.

Navigating news and clickbait is vital in a world overflowing with digital noise. By understanding the techniques behind clickbait and developing strategies to resist its allure, we can cultivate a more mindful and balanced relationship with the information we consume.

## Navigating the News Feed: Real vs. Ridiculous

Picture this: You're scrolling through your news feed, and you stumble upon a story claiming that scientists have taught cats to speak human languages, and they're planning a feline-led revolution. Absurd, right? But let's be honest—these days, it can be hard to tell what's real and what's just another fabricated headline intended to shock and entertain. The digital landscape is littered with news stories that blur the line between reality and fiction, making it crucial to assess the credibility of the sources we trust. The key is to cross-reference information with reputable outlets, ensuring that the stories we consume are grounded in fact rather than fiction. Consider it a bit like being on a treasure hunt, where the gold nuggets of truth are hidden among piles of fool's gold. Reputable sources have a history of journalistic integrity and transparency, which means they're less likely to peddle outrageous claims without solid evidence to back them up.

In this whirlwind of information, some news stories are so outlandish that they loop back around to being almost believable. Satirical news sites have mastered the art of weaving tales that, at first glance, seem plausible enough to be mistaken for genuine. Who hasn't been caught off guard by a satirical article shared by a friend, only to realize halfway through that the story's absurdity is the punchline? You might find yourself chuckling at a report about a politician proposing to paint all public buildings neon pink to boost national morale, only to remember that truth can sometimes be stranger than fiction. Then, there are the real headlines that sound like they should be satire, like when a city council accidentally approves a law banning ice cream trucks because someone misread the proposal. These stories highlight the fine line between comedy and reality, illustrating the importance of maintaining a healthy skepticism when reading the news.

But how do you verify the authenticity of a news story in a world where anyone with a computer can publish anything? Fact-checking websites and services are your best allies in this quest for truth. Platforms like FactCheck.org provide thorough analyses of claims circulating in the media, helping you easily separate fact from fiction. When evaluating a news source, consider its history and reputation. Has the outlet been known for reliable reporting, or does it have a track record of sensationalist headlines? It's also helpful to assess the presence of corroborating evidence. Are other reputable sources reporting the same story, or does it stand alone as a solitary voice in the digital wilderness? These tools and techniques can guide you through the noise, ensuring the information you consume is accurate and trustworthy.

Cultivating a mindset of skepticism and inquiry is vital in this age of information overload. Approach each piece of news with critical questions about its content and context. Who authored the article, and what might be their agenda? Are there potential biases at play? Encourage discussions that challenge assumptions and invite diverse perspectives. Engage in conversations with friends and family about the stories you encounter, fostering an environment where questioning is encouraged and assumptions are tested. This mindset sharpens your analytical skills and strengthens your ability to discern truth from misinformation.

As digital citizens, we have a responsibility to navigate the news feed with both curiosity and caution. By evaluating sources, verifying authenticity, and fostering critical thinking, we can enjoy the benefits of an informed perspective without falling victim to sensationalist tales or outright falsehoods. This approach allows us to engage with the world more thoughtfully, knowing that we can separate the real from the ridiculous in a landscape where the two often coexist in surprising harmony.

## Satire vs. Reality: The Thin Line of Misinformation

Ah, satire—the misunderstood cousin of news, often mistaken for its more serious counterpart. In a world where fake news and misinformation run rampant, satire cleverly disguises itself as truth, only to reveal its true purpose through a wink and a nod. Satirical news sites like The Onion have mastered this art, crafting headlines that dance on the edge of believability while holding up a mirror to society's absurdities. But why does satire exist? At its core, satire seeks to critique societal issues by exaggerating them to the point of ridiculousness. It's the class clown of journalism, using humor to highlight the flaws we often overlook. Yet, in a media landscape that's perpetually bombarding us with information, satire's subtle cues can sometimes be missed, leading to delightful confusion.

Take, for instance, the time when a satirical article went viral, convincing thousands that a local council had voted to replace its police force with community-trained llamas. Yes, you read that right —llamas. The piece, penned with tongue firmly in cheek, was meant to poke fun at the often outlandish solutions proposed in local politics. However, it quickly gained traction on social media, where the line between satire and reality blurred faster than a llama on the run. Reactions ranged from outrage to amusement, with many failing to realize the absurdity was intentional. It's a testament to how satire can be both a sharp tool for commentary and a source of unintentional hilarity when taken at face value.

So, how do you distinguish satire from actual news? It's all about recognizing the tone and style that define satirical content. Satire often employs hyperbole, irony, and absurdity to make its point, much like a stand-up comedian exaggerating a story to elicit laughs. Understanding the intent and context of a satirical piece is key. Is the headline too bizarre to be true? Are the characters and scenarios exaggerated to the point of implausibility? If you find yourself questioning the reality of a story, you're likely in the realm of satire. Knowing the usual suspects in the satirical world, like The Onion or The Babylon Bee, can also tell you when you're reading a well-crafted joke rather than a factual report.

Despite the potential for confusion, satire is valuable in encouraging critical reflection on current events. It serves as a tool for highlighting absurdities in real-world scenarios, prompting us to question the status quo. By presenting issues in an exaggerated light, satire invites us to step back and consider the underlying truths that might otherwise go unnoticed. It's a reminder that not everything should be taken at face value, urging us to dig deeper and seek the truth beneath the humor. Satire encourages an appreciation for both the humor and the lessons it imparts, reminding us that laughter can be a powerful catalyst for change.

As we wrap up this exploration of satire and its role in the media landscape, remember that the line between reality and satire can be thin, but it's not invisible. With a discerning eye and a sense of humor, you can navigate this terrain without falling into the trap of misinformation. Embrace the laughter and the lessons, and let them guide you toward a more informed and thoughtful perspective. As we move forward in our digital journey, let's carry these insights with us, ready to face the next challenge with clarity and an open mind.

SIX

# Mindful Tech Usage

Let me set the stage with this scene: I was at a quaint café where the barista knows your name and latte order by heart. I had just settled into my favorite corner, with the perfect view of the bustling street outside and the comforting hum of espresso machines inside. My laptop was closed—an intentional choice—and I was there to enjoy the rare pleasure of a tech-free afternoon. Or so I thought. As the aroma of freshly squeezed orange juice filled the air, I instinctively reached for my phone, only to remember I'd left it at home as part of my grand digital detox plan. Panic set in for a brief moment, followed by a liberating realization: I could actually experience the world without the constant stream of notifications vying for my attention.

## The Digital Detox Diaries

The concept of a digital detox might seem like a quaint notion from a bygone era, but in reality, it's a modern necessity. In our hyper-connected lives, taking a break from technology is like hitting the reset button for our minds. It's a deliberate pause from the barrage of digital inputs that often feel like a never-ending symphony of pings and alerts. The benefits are substantial, like a glass of freshly squeezed juice for the soul. Reduced stress and anxiety levels are among the first things people notice when they unplug. It's as if a weight lifts, allowing you to breathe more deeply and think more clearly. Improved concentration and productivity follow closely behind as the mental fog dissipates, replaced by a newfound clarity that enhances focus and creativity. A recent study supports this, showing that participants who limited social media use reported significant improvements in life satisfaction and stress levels.

Yet, as noble as the digital detox sounds, let's not pretend it's all smooth sailing. The road to a successful detox is often paved with humorous missteps. Take, for instance, the "accidental" reactivation of social media accounts. It's the digital equivalent of sleepwalking— one moment you're resolute in your decision to unplug, and the next, you've somehow found yourself knee-deep in a thread about the dietary habits of penguins. And then there's the irresistible compulsion to document your detox experience online. How ironic it is that in our quest to disconnect, we feel the urge to connect with others about how we're disconnecting. It's a modern paradox that many of us face and often results in entertaining tales of detox attempts gone awry.

Planning a successful digital detox requires a dash of strategy and a pinch of realism. Start by setting achievable goals and timelines. Instead of going cold turkey, begin with manageable increments, like an hour each evening without screens, gradually extending to longer periods. Identify tech-free zones and times, perhaps during meals or an hour before bed. These pockets of time can become sacred spaces for reflection, relaxation, and genuine connection with those around you. Enlist the support of family and friends who can hold you accountable and join you in the endeavor. After all, it's easier to resist the siren call of technology when you have allies on your side.

### *Case Study: Journaling the Digital Detox*

Laura, a social worker, felt more anxious and disconnected, constantly tethered to her phone for work emails, social media, and news updates. Realizing her digital habits were taking a toll, she started a digital detox journey, beginning with "tech-free Sundays." Laura documented her experiences in a journal to keep herself accountable, noting how each tech-free day affected her mood, focus, and relationships with family and friends. Initially, she struggled to check her phone, feeling a sense of FOMO. But over time, she began enjoying simple pleasures, like reading a physical book or going on long walks with her husband.

As weeks turned into months, Laura noticed meaningful changes: her mood was lighter, her focus sharper, and her relationships more connected. Her journal became a treasured guide, revealing the triggers that drew her back to her phone and the benefits of disconnecting. Inspired by her progress, she created a "digital balance manifesto," listing her intentions to maintain a healthier relationship with technology. This manifesto reminded her of the calm she found in tech-free moments and helped her commit to regular detox days. Laura's journey turned her journal into a tool of self-discovery and a roadmap for maintaining digital wellness.

**Lesson**: Laura's experience illustrates the power of journaling in fostering a balanced digital life. By documenting her detox journey, she was able to identify patterns, celebrate progress, and create a personal guide to digital mindfulness, helping her stay grounded in a tech-driven world.

### *Interactive Exercise: Your Detox Journey*

Consider starting a journal to document your digital detox journey. Reflect on your experiences during tech-free days and note any changes in mood, focus, or interactions with others. Use this journal to create a personal manifesto for digital balance, outlining your intentions and goals for a healthier relationship with technology.

Reflecting on your detox experiences offers valuable insights. A journal can become a cherished companion, capturing your thoughts and revelations as you navigate a world with fewer distractions. Through writing, you'll uncover patterns, identify triggers, and celebrate victories, no matter how small. As you do, consider creating a personal manifesto for digital balance—a guiding document that encapsulates your newfound understanding and commitment to a mindful, balanced digital life. This manifesto can remind you of the lessons learned and the path forward, helping you maintain a harmonious relationship with technology as you continue your journey through the digital landscape.

## Scroll Control: Mastering the Infinite Feed

There's a certain seductive quality to the infinite scroll that's hard to resist. It's like the digital version of potato chips—you can't stop at just one. You start by checking an innocent notification or a friend's post. You only find yourself 45 minutes later, knee-deep in a thread of cat videos followed by a meticulously detailed debate on the best way to fold a fitted sheet. The "just one more" mentality is the culprit here, a sneaky little voice in your head whispering that the next scroll will surely bring the content you've been searching for. This cycle is propelled by dopamine, the brain's feel-good chemical that rewards us with a tiny rush every time we encounter something entertaining or informative. Social media platforms know this well, utilizing endless feeds to keep us engaged, promising that the next swipe might reveal the ultimate piece of content or at least a passable meme.

But let's be honest: the humor in our scrolling habits is undeniable. Who hasn't fallen victim to the late-night rabbit hole of unrelated videos? You start with a tutorial on making sourdough bread and somehow end up watching a documentary on the migratory patterns of penguins. Or perhaps you've found yourself sitting in the same position for so long that you're not sure if your legs are still attached, only to realize that hours have passed without you noticing. These moments of absurdity are a testament to how easily time slips away when we're captivated by the digital world. And while it's amusing to recount these tales, they remind us of the subtle power that scrolling holds over our attention.

Adopting some practical methods to regain control over our scrolling habits is crucial. Start by setting time limits on your apps. Most smartphones now have features that allow you to monitor and limit your usage. Set a timer for your scrolling sessions, and when it goes off, take a moment to assess whether you've found what you were looking for or are simply wandering the digital aisles. Curate a feed that aligns with your interests and values. Unfollow accounts that no longer serve you and fill your feed with content that inspires or educates. By consciously choosing what appears on your screen, you can transform your scrolling into a more intentional and fulfilling experience.

But beyond just scrolling, there's a whole world waiting to be explored—one filled with activities that offer more satisfaction than the infinite feed ever could. Engaging in hobbies or creative projects is a wonderful way to break free from the scrolling cycle. Whether painting, gardening, writing, or woodworking, immersing yourself in a hands-on activity can provide a sense of accomplishment and joy that a screen simply cannot. Participating in social or community events is another fulfilling alternative. Join a local club, attend a workshop, or volunteer for a cause you're passionate about. These experiences enrich your life and foster connections with others, creating more lasting memories than any post or tweet.

In a world dominated by screens, finding fulfillment beyond the infinite feed is not only possible but deeply rewarding. By setting boundaries for our digital consumption and exploring the myriad of activities that lie beyond, we can regain control of our time and attention, discovering a more balanced and enriched life.

## Mindfulness in a Meme World

In today's digital age, memes have emerged as the quirky, hilarious, and sometimes nonsensical language of the internet, capturing the essence of modern communication. These bite-sized nuggets of humor and wit have become more than just entertainment—they reflect societal trends and mirror our collective consciousness. Whether it's a side-splitting take on a trending topic or a satirical jab at the latest political blunder, memes spread across platforms at lightning speed, reaching audiences far and wide. They've become a cultural phenomenon, transcending barriers and uniting people over shared laughter and understanding. As Paolo Gerbaudo describes, memes act as a digital culture's palette, painting vivid pictures of our hopes, anxieties, and desires.

But let's not kid ourselves; the line between enjoying memes and falling into the rabbit hole of procrastination is thinner than the latest iPhone. You sit down to catch up on work, and a meme about procrastination pops up, ironically delaying your tasks further. There's humor here, of course—the irony of using memes to avoid being mindful is not lost on anyone. Yet, this very humor can be a gentle nudge to remind us of the need for balance. Imagine scrolling through memes that make you chuckle and encourage mindfulness. Memes that promote digital wellness can turn a scroll session into a moment of reflection, offering light-hearted reminders to stay present and grounded. Creating such memes can be a fun and creative way to blend humor with mindfulness, encouraging others to pause and consider their digital habits.

Incorporating mindfulness into our digital interactions doesn't require completely overhauling our online behavior. It's about weaving small, intentional actions into our daily routines. Take mindful breaks during screen time—step away from your devices, stretch, and take a few deep breaths. This simple practice can rejuvenate your mind and body, reducing the sensory overload that often accompanies prolonged screen exposure. Practicing gratitude for online interactions is another powerful strategy. Instead of mindlessly scrolling, take a moment to appreciate the connection and information that digital platforms provide. Reflect on the positive exchanges and the knowledge gained, fostering a sense of gratitude that can enhance your online experiences.

Mindful creation and sharing of content is another avenue to explore. When you develop content that inspires reflection and discussion, you're not just contributing to the digital noise but adding value to the conversation. Share personal experiences highlighting the importance of being present, whether a photo capturing a serene moment in nature or a thoughtful caption accompanying a humorous meme. These snippets of authenticity can resonate deeply with others, encouraging them to reflect on their own lives and perhaps even inspire change. By fostering positivity and mindfulness in the content we share, we contribute to a more thoughtful and intentional digital community.

As we navigate this meme-driven digital landscape, it's essential to remember that while humor and entertainment are integral, they can coexist with mindfulness and intention. By finding the balance between indulging in light-hearted content and practicing mindful engagement, we can enjoy the best of both worlds without succumbing to the pitfalls of digital distractions. This chapter has explored how memes can be both a source of joy and a tool for mindfulness, highlighting the importance of intentional digital interactions. As we move forward, consider how you can incorporate these practices into your own digital life, creating a space where humor and mindfulness thrive side by side.

# SEVEN

# The Productivity Paradox

Picture this: you're at your desk with your green smoothie in hand, ready to conquer the day. You've got a playlist queued up, emails to answer, a presentation to prepare, and, for some reason, a sudden urge to reorganize your sock drawer. As you drink your smoothie, you decide to tackle everything at once, confident in your multitasking prowess. Fast forward an hour, and you find yourself staring at a half-written email trailing off mid-sentence, a presentation slide filled with more doodles than data, and socks strewn across your desk like confetti. Welcome to the chaotic world of multitasking, where the illusion of productivity often masks the reality of inefficiency.

Multitasking is like juggling flaming torches while riding a unicycle—impressive in theory, but mostly just a recipe for disaster. Despite its allure, the science is clear: multitasking is often less efficient than focusing on one task at a time. The concept of cognitive switching costs highlights this inefficiency. Each time you shift from one task to another, your brain incurs a "switching cost," a kind of mental toll that results in lost time and decreased focus. Instead of seamlessly flowing from task to task, you end up in a mental traffic jam, where your thoughts honk at each other for attention. The illusion of productivity comes from feeling busy, but in reality, you're just spreading your attention too thin.

Let's dive into the delightful chaos that is multitasking with some humor. Have you ever sent an email that trailed off into nonsense because your mind was elsewhere? "Dear Mr. Smith, I wanted to discuss the upcoming project and how we can... bananas and roller skates." Oops. Or perhaps you've found yourself mixing up work tasks with personal errands, like trying to schedule a Zoom meeting while also making a grocery list. It's all fun and games until you accidentally invite your boss to a potluck or tell a colleague you'd like to buy two dozen eggs. These mishaps are a testament to the brain's limitations, reminding us that even the most tech-savvy among us can fall prey to multitasking madness.

Scientific research backs up these amusing anecdotes. Studies have shown that multitasking often increases errors and wastes time as the brain struggles to process multiple information streams simultaneously. This juggling act also impacts memory retention and comprehension, leaving you with a jumbled mess of half-remembered facts and unfinished tasks. According to a study on cognitive control, heavy smartphone users frequently engaged in multitasking show higher error rates on cognitive tasks and lower sustained attention capacity. The irony here is that while we turn to multitasking to get more done, we often achieve the opposite, finding ourselves stuck in a cycle of inefficiency.

So, how do we break free from the multitasking trap and embrace the art of single-tasking? One effective technique is the Pomodoro Technique, which involves breaking your work into focused intervals, usually 25 minutes long, followed by a short break. This approach not only boosts concentration but also keeps fatigue at bay. A study comparing systematic breaks with self-regulated ones found that the former improved mood and efficiency, suggesting that the Pomodoro Technique can help you accomplish more in less time. Another strategy is creating a prioritization matrix, a simple tool to help you sort tasks by urgency and importance. By organizing your to-dos, you can tackle them individually, ensuring that your attention is fully dedicated to each task.

### *Case Study: From Multitasking Mayhem to Focused Productivity*

A project manager, Sophie was known for her ability to juggle multiple tasks—responding to emails, fielding calls, and updating project plans. But her "superpower" was starting to wear her down; she often felt mentally scattered and struggled to finish her work on time. Intrigued by the idea of single-tasking, Sophie decided to try the Pomodoro Technique. She set her timer for 25-minute intervals dedicated to one task at a time, with 5-minute breaks in between. At first, focusing on just one task felt odd, and she kept resisting the urge to check emails or messages. But by the end of the week, she noticed she was getting more done and felt less stressed.

Sophie tracked her progress in a journal, reflecting on the benefits of her new approach. She discovered that tasks she previously dreaded, like drafting reports, were more manageable when she tackled them uninterrupted. By the end of the week, her journal was filled with positive reflections on the power of focused work. Inspired by the impact on her productivity and well-being, Sophie committed to single-tasking for her most important tasks, using her journal to refine her approach. Her experiment with the Pomodoro Technique helped her realize that quality often matters more than quantity in achieving success.

**Lesson**: Sophie's journey illustrates the value of single-tasking in boosting focus, reducing stress, and enhancing productivity. By slowing down and embracing one task at a time, she could reclaim control over her workday and achieve a more balanced approach to productivity.

### *Interactive Exercise: Your Single-Tasking Plan*

Take a moment to reflect on your current work habits. Do you find yourself frequently multitasking? Consider trying the Pomodoro Technique for a week. Set a timer for 25-minute work intervals, followed by a 5-minute break. Keep a journal of your progress, noting any changes in focus, efficiency, or stress levels. Use this exercise to identify which tasks benefit most from single-tasking.

Ultimately, embracing single-tasking is about reclaiming focus and achieving true productivity. It's a shift in mindset, a move from multitasking chaos to a more mindful, intentional approach to work. So, next time you find yourself tempted to juggle a dozen tasks at once, remember the half-written emails and misplaced grocery lists. Give single-tasking a try—it might be the key to unlocking your full potential.

## Digital Distractions: Finding Focus in Chaos

Imagine sitting down at your desk, intent on tackling that project you've been putting off. You're armed with your favorite playlist, a steaming cup of whatever gets you through the morning, and a burning desire to get things done. But then, just as you're about to hit your stride, your phone buzzes with a notification. It's an email, a message, or perhaps just a reminder that your favorite influencer has posted another "life-changing" smoothie recipe. Before you know it, you're caught in a web of digital distractions, where every ping and pop-up feels like a personal affront to your productivity. It's a scenario that's all too familiar, a testament to the constant barrage of digital stimuli that vie for our attention every waking moment.

Let's face it, frequent email and message notifications are the digital equivalent of a toddler tugging at your sleeve, insistent and relentless.

They demand immediate attention, pulling you away from the task at hand and into a spiral of replies, forwards, and endless threads. Social media alerts and pop-ups are no better, seducing us with the promise of instant gratification and a quick dopamine hit. It's the classic "just one peek" trap—one minute you're checking a notification, and the next, you're deep into a thread debating whether dogs are better than cats, with no recollection of how you got there in the first place. These digital elements are masters at disrupting focus, turning our screens into a carnival of distractions that make concentrating on a single task feel like an Olympic sport.

There's a certain comedy in trying to work amidst this chaos. Picture yourself in the endless loop of opening and closing the same browser tabs, convinced that the next click will finally bring you back to where you started. Or maybe you find yourself staring blankly at your screen, having completely forgotten the original task that sent you spiraling down the rabbit hole of distraction. It's like going to the kitchen and forgetting why you went there, but with pixels and hyperlinks. These moments, while frustrating, are hilariously relatable, a shared experience in the modern age where focus feels as elusive as a Wi-Fi signal in a dead zone.

To combat this, creating a focus-friendly environment is key. Start by using website blockers during work hours to limit access to sites that are notorious for sucking you in. These digital bouncers keep you from wandering into the tempting void of endless content, allowing you to dedicate your attention to what truly matters. Establishing a dedicated, clutter-free workspace is another effective strategy. Clear your desk of unnecessary items, minimize digital clutter, and ensure your workspace is conducive to concentration. A clean, organized space can significantly reduce mental noise, helping you focus on the task at hand without the distraction of visual chaos.

Mindfulness techniques can also play a crucial role in maintaining concentration. Consider incorporating mindful breathing exercises into your routine to reset your focus. When distractions threaten to derail your productivity, take a moment to pause, close your eyes, and take a few deep breaths. This simple practice can clear your mind, reduce stress, and bring your attention back to the present moment. Setting intention before starting each task is another powerful tool. Before diving into a project, take a moment to define your goal and visualize the steps needed to achieve it. This intentional approach can anchor your focus, helping you navigate distractions more easily and clearly.

Finding focus requires combining practical strategies and mindful practices in the relentless chaos of digital distractions. By curating your environment and incorporating techniques that promote concentration, you can reclaim your attention and navigate the digital world with greater mindfulness and intention.

## The Procrastination Equation: Tech Edition

Procrastination. It's the classic nemesis of productivity, lurking in the shadows of every task list, waiting to pounce at the first sign of hesitation. In today's digital age, procrastination's arsenal has expanded, with an endless buffet of online distractions that seduce us from our goals. The internet is a vast entertainment playground, offering everything from the latest viral videos to endless streams of memes and social media updates. It's like an all-you-can-eat buffet where every dish is designed to keep you returning for just one more bite. The allure of endless entertainment can be overpowering. With just a click, you can escape the monotony of work and dive into an ocean of digital diversions.

A significant contributor to procrastination is the overwhelming task list, which often feels as daunting as climbing Everest without a sherpa. When faced with a mountain of tasks, retreating into the comfort of digital distractions is tempting. That to-do list resembles a horror movie script, where every unchecked box is a reminder of impending doom. So, what do we do? Rather than diving straight into our tasks, we often slip into the endless loop of "just one more" video, convincing ourselves that this next one will be the last before we get back to work. Spoiler alert: it rarely is. This is where procrastination wears its most charming disguise, presenting itself as a harmless indulgence while slyly eroding our time and focus.

Then there's the phenomenon of "productive procrastination." It's when you find yourself organizing files, color-coding spreadsheets, or tidying up your desktop, all under the pretense of preparing to work. It's the kind of procrastination that feels productive at the moment but ultimately leaves you with a pristine workspace and a still-looming deadline. It's like rearranging deck chairs on the Titanic—it looks good, but the ship is still sinking. We've all been there, convincing ourselves that these tasks are necessary preludes to productivity when, in reality, they're just glorified distractions.

But fear not, for breaking the procrastination cycle is possible. Start by setting specific, achievable goals. Instead of vague intentions like "work on project," break tasks into smaller, manageable pieces with clear deadlines. This reduces overwhelm and provides a roadmap to follow, making it easier to stay on track. Consider enlisting the help of accountability partners or apps to keep you honest. Share your goals with a friend or colleague who can check your progress and offer encouragement when you're tempted to stray. Digital tools like habit-tracking apps or productivity platforms can also serve as helpful nudges, reminding you of your commitments and celebrating your achievements, however small.

Interestingly, technology, often blamed for procrastination, can be leveraged to combat it. The rise of gamified productivity apps is a testament to this. For example, apps like Habitica turn task completion into a game, allowing you to earn rewards and level up as you accomplish your goals. This approach taps into our natural desire for achievement and progress, turning productivity into a fun and engaging experience. Other apps, like Trello or Asana, offer digital to-do lists where you can set deadlines, track progress, and visualize your workload. These tools help organize tasks and provide motivation through visual progress, making it easier to stay focused and productive.

Procrastination may be a formidable foe, but you can keep it at bay with the right strategies and tools. By setting clear goals, leveraging accountability, and embracing digital tools designed to enhance productivity, you can confidently turn the tide against procrastination and reclaim your time. As we wrap up this chapter on productivity, remember that the key to overcoming procrastination is not eliminating distractions entirely but managing them wisely. And with that, we'll venture into the complexities of digital relationships, exploring how our online interactions shape and influence our connections.

# EIGHT

# The AI Antics

Let me tell you about the time my smart speaker thought I was asking for a "moose playlist" when, in fact, I was just trying to set the mood with some smooth jazz. As you might imagine, my relaxing evening suddenly turned into the wild world of moose calls, echoing through my living room with an alarming authenticity. This delightful mishap is just one example of how artificial intelligence, for all its promises of perfection, often stumbles into the realm of the absurd. We live in an era where AI systems, despite their sophistication, are as susceptible to quirks and blunders as the rest of us.

Imperfect algorithms are a reminder that even machines can have off days. Take AI-generated art, for example. While some pieces are stunning, others look like Picasso and a malfunctioning printer had an unfortunate encounter. A painting created by AI might feature a human with three arms or a landscape where the sun rises from the ground instead of the horizon. These peculiar creations are not just amusing; they highlight the limitations of AI in understanding human aesthetics. According to an article from Bored Panda, AI art often struggles with creating realistic images of hands and faces, resulting in horrifying and hilarious outputs.

Then there's the world of natural language processing, where AI's attempts to grasp human language lead to comedic misinterpretations. You might send a voice command to your assistant, hoping for a quick weather update, only to receive a detailed account of some obscure historical battle. These misunderstandings aren't just limited to voice assistants. Autocorrect, another AI-driven tool, has turned many text messages into unintentional jokes. Who hasn't experienced the awkward moment when "Let's grab lunch" becomes "Let's grab a lynch"? These quirks remind us that while AI is impressive, it's not infallible.

Despite the hilarity of these machine-learning mishaps, there's a silver lining. Much like humans, AI systems learn and improve through trial and error. This iterative nature of training machine learning models means that AI gets slightly better with every mistake. It's like teaching a child to ride a bike—there will be wobbles and falls, but eventually, the balance is found. Each error provides valuable data, allowing the system to refine its algorithms and enhance its accuracy. This process of learning from mistakes makes AI a continually evolving technology, always on the cusp of its next breakthrough.

Interestingly, the imperfections of AI can also lead to unexpected opportunities for innovation. AI's errors sometimes spark creativity in ways we didn't anticipate. For instance, AI-generated music that veers off into unexpected harmonies or rhythms might inspire human composers to explore new musical territories. Similarly, AI art's bizarre interpretations of familiar subjects can push artists to rethink their approach and embrace abstract concepts. These happy accidents demonstrate that innovation isn't always born from precision and correctness; sometimes, the quirks and deviations pave the way for new ideas and perspectives.

### *Case Study: The Accidental AI Inspiration*

A high school art teacher, David was initially skeptical about incorporating AI into his creative process. However, he decided to experiment with using an AI art generator to brainstorm new ideas for his students. One day, he inputted a prompt for "a serene mountain landscape," hoping for a peaceful image he could use as a teaching reference. Instead, the AI produced a surreal image of a mountain made of clouds, with trees growing upside down and lakes floating mid-air. At first, David thought it was a glitch, but the strange, dreamlike scene unexpectedly sparked his creativity. He saw the potential to use the image in his lesson on surrealism, showing students how to find inspiration in unexpected places.

David's students were thrilled with the quirky artwork, and the surreal AI creation became the center of their project. As they worked, they laughed about the "happy accident" and explored how unconventional thinking can lead to exciting ideas. This minor AI mishap showed David and his students that art doesn't have to follow strict rules and that embracing imperfections can lead to some of the most memorable and inspiring moments. The experience transformed David's view of AI from a rigid tool to a creative collaborator, reminding him to welcome surprises in his art and life.

**Lesson**: David's experience highlights the value of embracing AI's quirks and imperfections as sources of inspiration. Sometimes, the most creative solutions come from letting go of expectations and being open to the "mistakes" technology can produce.

### *Interactive Exercise: Embracing AI's Quirks*

Take a moment to reflect on your own interactions with AI. Have there been moments when an AI's mistake was surprisingly helpful or inspiring? Consider how you might apply this mindset of embracing imperfection to other areas of your life. Jot down your thoughts and explore the potential for creativity that arises from the unexpected.

As we navigate the world of AI, it's important to remember that perfection isn't the ultimate goal. AI's quirks and imperfections remind us of the human element within technology, inviting us to laugh, learn, and innovate in ways we never thought possible. Through humor and understanding, we can appreciate AI's unique role in our lives, blending the mechanical with the magical in a dance that's as entertaining as it is enlightening.

## Robot Bias: When Algorithms Go Awry

Imagine asking your AI assistant to recognize a friend in a photo, only to have it confidently misidentify them as some obscure celebrity. This might seem like a harmless mix-up, yet it highlights a deeper issue: algorithmic bias. Like us, algorithms can develop biases, but instead of inheriting them from parents or society, they absorb them from the data they're fed. When these biases creep into AI systems, the societal implications can be significant. Take facial recognition software, for example. While it's fantastic for unlocking your phone with a glance, it struggles with recognizing the faces of people from diverse ethnic backgrounds. This isn't simply a technical glitch—it reflects the biases in the data used to train these systems. As a result, this technology can lead to misidentifications that disproportionately affect minority groups, raising concerns about privacy and equality.

Then, there are hiring algorithms designed to sift through countless resumes and select the best candidates. Sounds efficient, right? But these systems often inherit the biases of the very humans they aim to replace. In a notorious case, an algorithm used by a major tech company penalized resumes that included the word "women's," leading to gender bias in hiring decisions. It's a bit like having a robot butler who insists on serving cold soup because it once saw you eat gazpacho. Such biases not only perpetuate existing inequalities but also hinder diversity in the workplace.

Humor can be a powerful tool in highlighting the absurdity of biased algorithms. Picture an AI tasked with creating an equality-themed ad campaign. You'd expect it to showcase diversity, yet it features a lineup of identical mannequins, each with the same expressionless face. Or consider an AI that misinterprets cultural contexts, like assigning sombreros to everyone in a group photo simply because one person mentioned tacos. These scenarios, while amusing, underscore a crucial point: algorithms lack the contextual understanding that comes naturally to us.

Addressing bias in AI development starts with acknowledging the importance of diverse data sets and inclusive design. Just as a chef needs a variety of ingredients to craft a flavorful dish, AI requires a wealth of perspectives to function equitably. Collaborative efforts between developers and ethicists are vital. By bringing together diverse voices, we can identify potential biases and implement fairness checks that scrutinize AI models for unintended consequences. It's like having friends proofread your work—not only do they catch your typos, but they also ensure your message comes across clearly and fairly.

Promoting ethical AI practices means advocating for transparency and accountability. Open-sourcing AI models for public scrutiny is one way to achieve this. By allowing experts to examine the inner workings of algorithms, we can identify and correct biases before they cause harm. Educating AI developers on ethical considerations is equally essential. It's about cultivating a sense of responsibility and awareness so developers understand the broader impact of their creations. Imagine teaching a class of AI developers not only the technical skills they need but also the moral compass to guide their work.

As we navigate this ever-evolving landscape, it's crucial to recognize that AI is both a tool and a reflection of our values. By addressing bias and promoting fairness, we can ensure that AI is an ally in pursuing a more equitable world. Through collaboration, education, and a touch of humor, we can guide AI development toward a future where its potential is realized without compromising the principles we hold dear.

## AI in Everyday Life: The Unseen Puppeteer

Picture this: you're casually browsing an online store, idly considering whether those neon socks really match your vibe, when suddenly the screen suggests a pair of electric blue sneakers to complete the look. It's as if the internet knows you better than your best friend. Welcome to the world of AI, quietly orchestrating our decisions without us even noticing. Personalized shopping recommendations are just one of the many ways AI subtly weaves itself into the fabric of our daily lives. It's there in our phones, predicting the next word in our text messages with eerie accuracy, and it's in our inboxes, filtering out spam with the precision of a well-trained bouncer at a high-end nightclub. Even our morning commutes aren't immune from AI's touch. Those navigation systems that expertly steer us away from traffic jams are all thanks to algorithms working tirelessly behind the scenes. They're the unsung heroes of our daily routines, making life a little smoother, one recommendation at a time.

Yet, for all its cleverness, AI sometimes slips up in the most delightful ways. Have you ever asked your music app for a playlist to help you focus, only to be serenaded by an unexpected mix of heavy metal and mariachi? Or perhaps, like me, you've witnessed your smart home devices holding a conversation, seemingly plotting their next move while you watch with bemused fascination. In these moments, AI's pervasive presence becomes humorously evident, reminding us that even the most advanced technology can have a mind of its own—or at least pretend to. These instances provide a good chuckle and a gentle reminder that while AI is intelligent, it's still navigating the intricacies of human preferences and behaviors.

The convenience AI provides comes with its own set of concerns, primarily around privacy. Every personalized recommendation is built on data, your data. It's like having an invisible assistant taking notes on your every whim and fancy, ready to serve the perfect ad or suggestion at the right moment. The trade-off between convenience and privacy is a delicate one. On one hand, AI makes our lives easier and more efficient.

On the other hand, it raises questions about how much we're willing to share with our digital companions. The implications of data-driven personalization are vast, touching on everything from targeted ads to the potential for misuse of personal information. Managing digital footprints becomes paramount in this context. It's about being aware of the trails we leave behind and taking steps to minimize them, like adjusting privacy settings, opting out of data sharing where possible, and being mindful of the information we voluntarily provide.

Looking ahead, AI's role in our lives is poised to expand in fascinating ways. Imagine AI companions with distinct personalities, like a digital sidekick learning your quirks and tailoring interactions to suit your mood. Or consider AI-driven innovations in healthcare, where algorithms could assist doctors in diagnosing conditions with unprecedented accuracy, potentially saving lives. AI could personalize educational learning experiences, adapting curriculums to fit each student's pace and style. These possibilities are both exciting and daunting, offering a glimpse into a future where AI is more than just a tool—it's a partner in our daily endeavors.

As we ponder this future, it's important to approach AI with a blend of curiosity and caution. The potential benefits are immense, but so are the challenges, particularly around ethics and privacy. By staying informed and engaged, we can confidently navigate this evolving landscape, ensuring that AI serves as a force for good in our lives. As we transition to the next chapter, consider how AI shapes your world today and how it might transform it tomorrow.

# NINE

# Digital Relationships Deconstructed

Picture this: you're standing at a party, drink in hand, when someone you've never met approaches you with a grin and a wink. Before you can say a word, they whip out a business card that reads, "Swipe Right for a Good Time." Welcome to the parallel universe of dating apps, where the all-too-familiar thumb flick has replaced traditional courtship rituals. In the span of a decade, dating apps have turned the world of romance on its head, transforming the art of meeting someone special into a digital game of chance. What used to require courage, a well-timed compliment, and perhaps a dash of charm now hinges on the mastery of crafting the perfect profile and nailing the art of the opening line. Dating apps have become more than just platforms; they're cultural phenomena, reshaping expectations and practices and, in some cases, our entire approach to love.

The evolution of dating apps can be traced back to when finding love online seemed as outlandish as finding a unicorn in your backyard. Yet, here we are in a world where swiping left or right is as natural as breathing. The rise of swiping culture has introduced us to the concept of instant judgments, where a single photo or a clever bio can make or break a potential connection. Profiles have morphed into digital resumes, carefully curated to highlight our most appealing traits while conveniently glossing over that we occasionally eat cereal for dinner. According to a study by the Pew Research Center, 30% of U.S. adults have tried online dating, with many reporting positive experiences.

But let's not forget the humor inherent in this digital dating dance. Misleading profile pictures are as old as time—or at least as old as Instagram filters. You think you're meeting someone with a jawline sharp enough to cut glass, only to find that the person before you could have a side gig as a professional catfish. And then there's the phenomenon of ghosting, where a promising match vanishes into the digital ether, leaving you wondering if they were ever real in the first place. It's like watching a magic trick where the rabbit disappears but never reappears, leaving you with nothing but an empty hat and a pang of bewilderment.

Despite the quirks and pitfalls, dating apps offer a unique opportunity to foster genuine connections—if you know how to navigate them. Crafting an honest and engaging profile is the first step in attracting the right kind of attention. Be authentic, but not too authentic; no one needs to know about your collection of novelty socks just yet. Prioritize meaningful conversations over small talk, diving into topics that spark curiosity and connection. And when the time feels right, set intentions for offline meetups. After all, the ultimate goal is to transition from screens to reality, where you can truly get to know someone beyond the confines of text boxes and emojis.

Balancing digital and real-life interactions is crucial in building a relationship that stands the test of time. Planning activities that encourage conversation—like a casual walk in the park or a visit to an art exhibit—can provide a natural backdrop for connection without the pressure of a formal dinner. Recognizing red flags during in-person meetings is equally important; trust your instincts if something feels off. Sometimes, that charming wit online doesn't quite translate in person, and that's okay. It's all part of the process of finding someone who truly complements you.

### *Case Study: Designing the Perfect First Date*

James, a 32-year-old graphic designer, was feeling burnt out by typical online dates that seemed to follow the same routine—coffee shops, small talk, and polite goodbyes. Wanting to break the cycle, he decided to try an exercise to envision his ideal first date. He thought about activities that would allow for genuine conversation without the usual pressure of a formal setting. After brainstorming, James imagined a low-key evening: a trip to a local art exhibit (where he could share his passion for design), a relaxed walk through a nearby park, and a stop at a quirky food truck.

Excited to try his new approach, James added these ideas to his dating profile as conversation starters, clarifying that he valued creativity and meaningful interaction. Soon, he met someone interested in his unique idea for a first date. The experience was a refreshing change—both he and his date felt more at ease, with plenty to talk about and no need for forced small talk. James realized that creating a date aligned with his personality helped him connect more authentically, transforming the typical dating experience into something memorable.

**Lesson**: James's story shows that crafting an ideal first date can lead to more meaningful connections. By thoughtfully planning activities that reflect his personality and values, he fostered a genuine, enjoyable experience, setting a positive tone for future dates.

### *Interactive Exercise: Craft Your Ideal First Date*

Take a moment to envision your ideal first date. Consider both online and offline elements that would create a meaningful experience. Jot down a few activities that foster genuine conversation and connection, and reflect on how you can incorporate these ideas into your dating life.

In a world where digital dating is the new norm, it's important to approach it with an open mind, a sense of humor, and a willingness to embrace both the triumphs and the mishaps. The journey to finding love may look different than it did for previous generations, but it remains a journey worth taking—swipes, quirks, and all.

## The Relationship Status Update: It's Complicated

Imagine scrolling through social media on a lazy Sunday afternoon when you spot an update from a friend: "In a Relationship." It is an innocuous declaration, yet it sends ripples across their digital network, sparking a flurry of likes, heart emojis, and congratulatory comments. Suddenly, a simple relationship status becomes a public spectacle, dissected and analyzed by everyone from your college roommate to that distant cousin who always shares questionable memes. Social media has turned what was once a private matter into a public performance, where the perception of a relationship is often shaped by the number of likes a post receives or the comments it garners. The digital world has a funny way of amplifying what was once whispered over coffee into something broadcast to the masses.

These public declarations can complicate relationships in ways we never anticipated. You might feel compelled to update your status to match your partner's, lest the world assumes there's trouble in paradise. That relationship timeline becomes a digital testament to your love, scrutinizing each change like a plot twist in a popular TV series. And then there's the impact of likes and comments, where each heart and "Congrats!" becomes a currency of validation, turning personal milestones into public events. The pressure to maintain a perfect relationship image online is immense, often making couples more concerned about how things appear rather than how they actually feel.

There's a hilarious awkwardness in managing relationships online that's hard to ignore. Oversharing personal details in public posts can be both entertaining and cringe-worthy. We've all seen those couples who document every date night or spat, turning their love story into a soap opera for all to see. It's like watching a reality show unfold on your feed, except the stars are your friends, and the plotlines are as predictable as a sitcom rerun. The pressure to present a picture-perfect relationship can lead to comically staged photos, where smiles are plastered while tensions simmer outside the frame. It's a reminder that what we see online often bears little resemblance to reality, where messy, beautiful imperfections live.

Navigating these digital relationship challenges requires foresight and humor. Setting boundaries for social media interactions is a good starting point. Decide with your partner what parts of your relationship you're comfortable sharing and what should remain between you. This might mean agreeing to keep certain milestones or disagreements offline or limiting how often you post about each other. Discussing your online presence with partners or friends can help ensure mutual understanding and prevent misunderstandings. Open communication about social media boundaries fosters trust and respect, reducing the likelihood of digital faux pas that can lead to real-world tension.

Enhancing privacy and maintaining authenticity in relationships amidst digital pressures is crucial. Consider keeping intimate moments offline, cherishing them as special memories rather than public broadcasts. It's about savoring the laughter and tears without needing an audience, allowing your relationship to grow organically without the weight of digital expectations. Focus on personal growth over online appearances, prioritizing the quality of your interactions rather than their online portrayal. After all, the most meaningful connections are often forged away from the screens, in the quiet moments that go unshared but are deeply felt.

Digital relationships can be a rollercoaster of emotions, humor, and unexpected twists. As you navigate this landscape, remember that it's okay to have fun with it, to laugh at the absurdities, and to cherish the authentic connections that thrive beyond the pixels. Each relationship is unique, and finding a balance between online sharing and offline intimacy can lead to a richer, more fulfilling experience. So whether you're updating your status or sharing a candid moment, keep it genuine, light, and real.

## From "DM" to "IRL": Bridging the Digital Divide

We live in a time when relationships often begin with the tap of a screen, a digital handshake that somehow feels personal and distant. It's all well and good to exchange messages with your new friend or romantic interest, but there comes a point when emojis and GIFs just won't cut it. Moving from digital to face-to-face interactions is crucial for building trust and rapport. In person, you can read body language, hear the warmth in someone's voice, and even share a laugh over how much taller (or shorter) you are than expected. Text-based communication, while convenient, has its limitations. It lacks the nuances of tone and expression, often leading to misunderstandings. A sarcastic remark, for instance, can easily be mistaken for genuine criticism in a chat. Meeting in person allows you to connect on a deeper, more authentic level, where a shared smile can say more than a thousand words.

Of course, transitioning from the digital world to real life isn't always smooth sailing. Imagine the scene: you've spent weeks chatting with someone, only to find yourself awkwardly standing in line at Starbucks for a Frappuccino, desperately searching for a conversation starter that isn't, "So, do you like Frappuccino?" It's like a sitcom where the two main characters finally meet and everything goes hilariously awry.

Perhaps the confident wit displayed in text doesn't quite translate, or maybe that inside joke about pineapples on pizza just doesn't land the same way in person. These moments can be awkward, but they're also strangely endearing, reminders that real life is deliciously unpredictable. Misunderstandings from digital conversations can also surface, leading to some comedic exchanges. You thought they loved hiking, but it turns out they meant "liking" as in casually appreciating the idea from the comfort of their couch. These quirks are part of the charm of moving offline, where the imperfections make the experience all the more genuine.

So, how do you successfully bridge this digital divide? Start by planning low-pressure meetups in public spaces. A casual stroll through a park or a trip to a local cafe provides a relaxed environment where you can focus on each other without the pressure of a formal setting. Establishing common interests to discuss offline can also pave the way for meaningful interactions. Whether it's a shared love for art, a mutual interest in photography, or a passion for trying new cuisines, these topics can break the ice and offer a natural flow to the conversation. Remember, the goal isn't to replicate your online chats but to create new, shared experiences that bring you closer.

But what about the couples separated by miles, relying on technology to bridge the gap? Long-distance relationships have their own set of challenges, yet technology can be a lifeline. Regular video calls and virtual dates can help maintain a sense of presence, allowing you to share moments and keep the connection alive. Plan visits whenever possible, even if it's just for a weekend, to reinforce the bond in person. Shared experiences, whether binge-watching a series together over a video call or exploring a new city hand-in-hand, strengthen the relationship and create a tapestry of memories to draw upon during lonely times.

The digital world offers endless possibilities for connection, but the magic truly happens when we take the leap into real-life interactions. Whether you're navigating the quirks of an in-person meeting or finding creative ways to bridge the distance, these experiences enrich our relationships and remind us of the joy of human connection. As we continue to explore the complexities of digital relationships, remember that while technology facilitates connection, it's the moments beyond the screen that truly matter.

With these insights, we're ready to move forward and explore new facets of our digital lives. As we transition into the next chapter, let's carry these lessons with us, ready to embrace the challenges and rewards of living in a tech-driven world.

TEN

# Self-Improvement in a Digital Age

Have you ever found yourself pacing around your living room, phone in hand, trying to squeeze out those last few steps to meet the elusive goal of 10,000 steps? I once caught myself walking in circles, dodging furniture with the grace of a sleepwalker, just to see my smartwatch light up with digital fireworks. Welcome to the world of the Quantified Self, where every step, heartbeat, and REM cycle is meticulously tracked, analyzed, and sometimes overanalyzed. This movement, rooted in the idea of self-surveillance, promises to turn our daily lives into a series of data points that can guide us to better health, productivity, and happiness—or so it claims.

In the age of self-tracking, wearable fitness devices are the modern-day oracle, predicting everything from our calories burned to the quality of our sleep. Wearable fitness trackers, like smartwatches, have become our digital personal trainers, constantly nudging us to move more, sit less, and occasionally, breathe. Smart scales now do more than just tell us our weight; they plunge into the depths of body composition analysis, revealing things about our muscle mass and fat percentage that we never asked to know. And let's not forget about sleep monitors, those nifty gadgets that promise insights into our sleep patterns. They're like the nosy neighbors of the tech world, peeking into our dreams and reporting back with charts and graphs that suggest why we might be waking up grumpy.

Habit trackers are the unsung heroes of this movement, offering a visual diary of our daily rituals, from flossing to meditation, in colorful charts and streaks that provide a sense of accomplishment. They're like the digital equivalent of gold stars in a kindergarten classroom, rewarding us for brushing our teeth or drinking enough water. But here's where the humor kicks in: sometimes, the pursuit of self-quantification takes a turn for the absurd. Ever found yourself competing with friends on fitness leaderboards, only to realize you've been pacing in a circle for ten minutes to out-step a coworker who's blissfully unaware of the competition? Or perhaps you've felt the pressure of a fitness tracker urging you to take another lap around the kitchen as if your evening snack depended on it?

These scenarios are comically familiar, yet they reveal a deeper truth: while data-driven gadgets can motivate us, they can also lead to what some call "health data anxiety." This term refers to the stress and obsession that can arise from constant monitoring, where the numbers become less of a guide and more of a judgment. According to a study, wearable technology can exacerbate mental health issues, especially when users feel pressured to meet or exceed set goals, leading to unnecessary medical visits. It's like having a nagging digital conscience that tracks your every move and whispers, "You could do better."

So, how do we strike a balance between helpful data and over-reliance on numbers? One way is to listen to your body and trust your intuition, even when your gadgets suggest otherwise. If your smartwatch tells you to run a marathon, but your legs are screaming, "Please, no," it might be time to take a rest day. Remember, you are not a data point; you are a complex, intuitive being capable of understanding when to push forward and rest. It's important to avoid using numbers as the sole measure of self-worth or success. A dip in your sleep score doesn't define your day, nor does a missed step goal make you any less accomplished.

For those looking to enhance personal growth with tech, plenty of gadgets and apps are designed to support your journey. For instance, meditation apps with biometric feedback can help you track your stress levels and guide you toward a more mindful state. Nutrition apps offer insights into caloric intake and macros, making aligning your diet with your wellness goals easier. These tools are like digital companions, offering gentle nudges toward better habits without the pressure of perfection.

### *Case Study: Trusting Intuition Over Data*

Rachel, a fitness enthusiast, was a dedicated user of self-tracking gadgets. From her smartwatch to her food-tracking app, she relied on data to guide her workouts, sleep schedule, and diet. She'd check her daily stats religiously, celebrating when she hit her targets and feeling frustrated on days when the numbers fell short. One weekend, Rachel went on a hiking trip without cell service and realized her watch wasn't tracking her steps or heart rate. Initially, she felt anxious about not meeting her "daily goals," but as the day went on, she found herself more relaxed and present, enjoying the hike without the pressure of hitting a number.

After this experience, Rachel began reflecting on areas where she might rely too heavily on data instead of tuning into her body's natural cues. She realized she often ignored signs of exhaustion because her stats didn't show that she'd "worked hard enough." Inspired by this insight, Rachel decided to reserve one "tech-free" workout day each week, focusing on how she felt rather than on numbers. Over time, she enjoyed her activities more and felt a stronger connection to her body's needs, reminding her that sometimes intuition can be a better guide than data alone.

**Lesson**: Rachel's journey shows the importance of balancing self-tracking with personal intuition. She regained a sense of freedom and well-being by allowing herself to step away from data occasionally, proving that self-improvement doesn't always have to be measured in numbers.

***Interactive Exercise: Finding Your Balance***

Take a moment to reflect on your relationship with self-tracking gadgets. Are there areas where you feel overly dependent on the data they provide? Jot down a few thoughts or examples where intuition might serve you better than numbers. Consider how you can integrate these insights into your daily routine, creating a more balanced and mindful approach to self-improvement.

As we embrace the potential of self-quantification, let's remember the importance of intuition and humor in our pursuit of growth. After all, life isn't just a series of data points; it's a journey filled with surprises, laughter, and the occasional detour around the living room furniture.

## Tech-Savvy Habits: Turning Apps into Allies

Imagine a world where your phone doesn't just help you waste time but actually helps you make the most of it. Enter habit-tracking apps, your new best friends in the quest for self-improvement. These digital companions are designed to keep you on track with everything from drinking water to learning a new language. They use reminders and streaks to motivate you, turning daily tasks into a game of sorts. Each time you complete a habit, you get a satisfying checkmark or badge, a small victory in the grand scheme of personal growth. Then there are the goal-setting apps with customizable milestones, letting you break down big ambitions into bite-sized pieces that are easier to tackle.

Yet, as with any relationship, there are ups and downs. Habit apps can be hilariously passive-aggressive. Miss logging a habit, and you might receive a notification that's equal parts reminder and guilt trip: "It's been three days since you last flossed. Are you sure you're doing okay?" These little nudges are meant to keep us accountable, but sometimes, they feel more like that friend who won't stop nagging you about joining their gym. Then, there's the joy of celebrating small victories. Some apps throw virtual confetti at you for completing a task, turning the mundane into a mini celebration. It's like having a cheerleader in your pocket, albeit one that wants you to remember to hydrate.

Choosing the right app is crucial for ensuring it aligns with your personal goals. Look for user-friendly interfaces and customizable settings, making it easy to tailor the app to your needs. Scour the reviews and check for proven effectiveness. After all, you want a tool that's been tried and tested, not just one with a catchy logo. Consider how well the app integrates with your existing tools and platforms. A seamless experience across devices can make a world of difference when you're trying to maintain new habits.

Maintaining motivation is often the biggest hurdle in forming new habits. Technology can be your ally here, offering ways to stay engaged and committed. Joining online communities related to your goals can provide invaluable support and accountability. Whether it's a group dedicated to daily meditation or a forum for novice runners, connecting with others on a similar path can keep you inspired. It's like the digital version of a support group, minus the awkward circle of folding chairs.

Setting realistic expectations is another key strategy. It's all too easy to get caught up in the excitement of a new habit and set goals that are too ambitious. Start small and celebrate incremental progress. Each step forward is worth acknowledging, even if it feels minor. Remember, it's about building momentum and creating a sustainable routine. Avoid the trap of all-or-nothing thinking, which can lead to burnout and discouragement.

Incorporating humor into your habit-building process can also lighten the load. Laughing at the inevitable slip-ups and challenges makes the journey more enjoyable. Didn't meet your goal today? No worries—there's always tomorrow, and maybe there will be a funny story to share with fellow strugglers. Embrace the messiness of growth, knowing that perfection is overrated and imperfection is what makes us human.

The intersection of technology and self-improvement is a fascinating space full of possibilities for growth and change. By leveraging the power of habit-tracking and goal-setting apps, you can transform your digital devices into powerful tools for positive change. It's all about finding the right balance, staying motivated, and enjoying the ride with a healthy dose of humor to keep things in perspective.

## Personal Growth with a Punchline

There's something inherently absurd about self-improvement, isn't there? It's a bit like trying to redecorate a house while still living in it —messy, chaotic, and occasionally hilarious. Infusing humor into the process can make personal growth feel less like a chore and more like an adventure. Take the trials of self-improvement, for instance. We've all been there, ready to conquer the world, only to find ourselves tangled in the mundane. Perhaps you've decided to meditate every morning, imagining a serene yoga studio but ending up in a living room cluttered with last night's pizza boxes. The comedy lies in these moments of contradiction, where our lofty aspirations meet the reality of everyday life. Using humor to navigate these situations makes them more bearable and builds resilience by allowing us to laugh at our own follies.

Goal setting is another area ripe for comedic exploration. Consider the perennial struggle with New Year's resolutions, those promises we make to ourselves with a sparkle of hope and a hint of naivety. We start January with grand ambitions fueled by the optimism of a new beginning. But by February, many of those goals have quietly disappeared, like socks in a dryer, never to be seen again. The irony here is palpable: we set these lofty goals, only to realize that the everyday demands of life—work, health, and relationships—have their own plans. Humor helps us see the absurdity of trying to stick to rigid plans amid life's unpredictable nature. It's a gentle reminder that while goals are important, flexibility is key, and sometimes, the best-laid plans need a good laugh to survive.

Laughing at setbacks can be a powerful tool for growth. When things don't go as planned—and let's be honest, they often don't—there's a choice to be made. We can wallow in frustration or see the humor in our missteps and learn from them. Embracing imperfection and resilience means accepting that mistakes are part of the process, not the end. Imagine you're baking a cake and using salt instead of sugar in a moment of distraction. Sure, it's a setback, but it's also a funny story to tell. By reframing failures as stepping stones to success, we find the courage to keep moving forward, knowing that each stumble brings us closer to our goals.

Cultivating a growth mindset is about more than just bouncing back from setbacks; it's about seeing challenges as opportunities for development. This perspective shift transforms how we approach obstacles, turning them into valuable lessons rather than roadblocks. Celebrating effort and progress over perfection is crucial in this endeavor. It's about acknowledging the small victories, like finally running that extra mile or mastering a new skill, even if it took a few tries. Humor plays a role here, too, offering a lighthearted lens through which to view our efforts. It reminds us that growth is a journey, not a destination and that the occasional detour or laugh along the way is all part of the experience.

As we wrap up this chapter on personal growth, remember that humor is an ally in your self-improvement journey. It lightens the load, keeps things in perspective, and makes the process a little more enjoyable. Let humor guide you, whether you're setting goals, facing setbacks, or cultivating a growth mindset. After all, life is too short to take too seriously. Embrace the punchlines, find joy in the journey, and keep moving forward with a smile.

In the next chapter, we'll explore the fascinating world of tech-induced stress and its solutions, delving into strategies for maintaining mental balance in a digital age.

ELEVEN

# Tech-Induced Stress and Solutions

I knew I had hit my digital breaking point when, during a heated debate with my smart fridge about the merits of kale vs. iceberg lettuce, my phone buzzed with another notification: "Your screen time was up 22% last week." It was official; my technology was tattling on me. Here I was, juggling emails, social media updates, and a growing pile of unanswered messages, all while my fridge was trying to get in on the healthy eating trend. It was a stark reminder of how constant connectivity can sneak up on us, like a cat that silently appears on your keyboard during a Zoom meeting.

## The Anxiety Algorithm: When Tech Turns Toxic

In our hyper-connected world, it's no surprise that tech-induced anxiety has become a familiar companion for many. The pressure to be "always on" permeates our lives, turning us into digital marionettes dancing to the tune of every ping and buzz. It's a landscape where putting your phone down feels like an act of rebellion. The flood of notifications and updates is relentless, each demanding our immediate attention as if the world might stop spinning if we don't reply to that group chat about next weekend's plans. This state of perpetual alertness can lead to a unique form of decision fatigue, where the sheer volume of content choices leaves us paralyzed, like a deer caught in the headlights of the information superhighway.

The comedic side of tech stress often plays out in those small, absurd moments that pepper our days. Take, for instance, the widespread panic that ensues when your phone's battery hits the dreaded 1%. It's a crisis of modern proportions, triggering frantic searches for a charger as if life itself might cease when the screen goes dark. Or consider the mental gymnastics we perform after misreading an email, imagining worst-case scenarios where a typo could lead to international incidents. While amusing in hindsight, these moments highlight how deeply technology has entwined itself with our psyche, turning minor mishaps into sources of significant stress.

But how does all this digital chaos affect us biologically? It's a question worth exploring, as the physiological responses to tech stress mirror those triggered by more traditional stressors. Prolonged screen time can lead to elevated cortisol levels, the body's primary stress hormone, affecting everything from sleep to mood. And let's not forget the impact of blue light, that insidious glow from our devices that tricks our brains into thinking it's still daytime, even as the clock ticks toward midnight. This light disrupts our sleep patterns and contributes to mental strain, creating a vicious cycle of stress and exhaustion.

To combat tech-induced anxiety, it's essential to establish boundaries that allow for mental reprieve. One effective strategy is implementing tech-free times or zones within your daily routine. Consider designating certain hours of the day, such as during meals or before bedtime, as technology-free periods. This practice can reduce the constant barrage of digital demands, providing a much-needed break for both mind and body. Similarly, creating physical spaces where technology is not welcome in your home can foster a sense of calm and encourage more mindful interactions.

Another powerful tool in the fight against tech stress is digital decluttering. Just as a cluttered room can lead to a cluttered mind, a chaotic digital environment can exacerbate overwhelming feelings. Take time to organize your digital spaces, delete unnecessary apps and files, and streamline your notifications to focus only on what's truly important. This simplification can create a clearer mental landscape, reducing anxiety and improving focus.

Finally, setting realistic expectations for response times for yourself and others is crucial. Permitting yourself to delay responses can be liberating in a world prioritizing immediacy. Communicate your availability to friends and colleagues, letting them know when you'll be offline and when they can expect a reply. This transparency alleviates the pressure of constant connectivity and fosters healthier relationships by establishing clear boundaries.

### *Case Study: Creating a Tech-Free Sanctuary*

Tom, a software developer, was finding it increasingly difficult to unplug. With his phone constantly buzzing with notifications, he often felt like he had never fully "clocked out" from work. He recognized the need for change and designed his bedroom as a tech-free zone. He imagined it as a sanctuary dedicated to relaxation, free from the endless pull of screens. To make this happen, Tom removed his phone charger from the bedroom, replaced his alarm clock with a non-digital one, and set a rule: no screens allowed after 9 p.m. Instead of his usual phone-scrolling routine, he stocked his bedside table with a few books he'd wanted to read.

The first few nights were challenging, as Tom was itching to check his messages before bed. But as the days passed, he noticed a significant difference in his sleep quality and mood. His bedroom gradually became a place of calm, and he began looking forward to his screen-free evenings. Tom found that unwinding with a book helped him fall asleep more easily, and he woke up feeling refreshed. Creating this tech-free sanctuary allowed Tom to decompress from the demands of his digital world, giving him a space where he could truly recharge.

**Lesson**: Tom's experience illustrates the benefits of setting intentional tech-free zones. By creating a dedicated space for relaxation and unplugging, he reduced his stress and improved his sleep, showing that simple changes can foster greater balance and well-being in a tech-heavy world.

### *Interactive Exercise: Craft Your Tech-Free Zone*

Take a moment to envision what your ideal tech-free zone might look like. Is it your dining room, where meals can be enjoyed without the interruption of screens, or perhaps your bedroom, transformed into a sanctuary of rest? Create a plan to implement this space, considering factors such as time of day and the activities you'll pursue instead. Reflect on how these changes might impact your stress levels and overall well-being.

By embracing these strategies, you can begin to untangle yourself from the web of tech-induced anxiety, finding balance and peace in a world that often feels anything but.

## Laughing at Stress: Humor as a Digital De-stressor

I once found myself in a virtual meeting where the only attendees were myself, a stray cat that wandered across my keyboard, and a glitchy connection that made my voice sound like a robot on helium. It was a moment that could have been stressful, but instead, I burst out laughing. This was a reminder of how humor can be a powerful antidote to the stress that technology sometimes brings into our lives. Laughter has this unique ability to shift our perspective, turning tense situations into moments of shared humanity. It lightens the mood, setting off a chain reaction of joy that can ripple through our day, reducing stress and even improving our physical health by lowering blood pressure and releasing endorphins. It's like nature's way of gifting us a reset button that doesn't require a Wi-Fi connection.

Everyday tech mishaps provide a treasure trove of opportunities for laughter. Consider the classic autocorrect blunder, where a simple message of "I'll be there in a sec" morphs into something entirely unintended—like "I'll be there in a duck." Suddenly, you're frantically explaining to a friend that you're not planning to arrive with a waterfowl. Or picture those moments in virtual meetings when a colleague's child decides it's the perfect time to showcase their latest dance move right behind their unsuspecting parent in the middle of a serious presentation. While initially disconcerting, these scenarios can become humorous anecdotes we share with friends, turning potential stress into a source of connection and camaraderie.

Incorporating humor into our digital interactions can serve as a buffer against the pressures of modern life. One way to achieve this is by following comedy accounts or subscribing to humorous newsletters. These little bursts of joy can brighten your inbox or social media feed, providing a welcome distraction from more serious content. You might also consider using memes or funny videos as stress-busters. A well-timed meme has the power to turn a frown upside down, offering a lighthearted take on the universal struggles we all face. Sharing these moments with friends online can foster a sense of community, reminding us that we're all in this digital whirlwind together.

Building a humor habit doesn't require a stand-up comedy routine or a stockpile of jokes. It's about nurturing a mindset that seeks out the funny side of life's challenges. Keeping a journal of daily humorous experiences can be a delightful way to capture those moments that make you smile. Whether it's a witty comment overheard at the grocery store or a personal mishap that had you in stitches, recording these snippets of joy can help you cultivate an appreciation for life's lighter moments. Engaging in activities that naturally evoke laughter—like watching a favorite comedy show or playing a silly game with friends—can also reinforce this habit, ensuring laughter becomes a regular part of your digital and real-life routines.

With the constant barrage of digital demands, finding humor in technology's quirks can be a lifeline. It's about allowing ourselves to step back and see the hilarity in what might otherwise be a pressure cooker of stress. So, the next time technology throws you a curveball, take a moment to pause, chuckle, and embrace the silliness of it all. After all, laughter might just be the best app you ever downloaded.

## Rebooting the Brain: Stress Relief in a Screen-Filled World

Let's face it. Our screens have become our constant companions, always within arm's reach, whispering (or rather, buzzing) sweet nothings—or, more accurately, stressful demands—into our ears. You're not alone if you've ever found yourself rubbing your eyes, pondering whether you've developed a superpower to read blurry text. This, my friends, is digital eye strain, a charming side effect of spending too much time staring at your phone, computer, or tablet. Symptoms include dry eyes, blurred vision, and headaches that make you question your life choices. But digital eye strain is only the tip of the iceberg. When our brains juggle the cognitive load of multitasking on screens, we experience mental exhaustion. It's like running a marathon without leaving your chair, only to collapse into a heap of fractured attention spans and forgotten to-do lists.

In response to this overload, many of us have developed dramatic rituals to escape the clutches of screen fatigue. Picture this: you're shutting down your laptop with the exaggerated flair of a soap opera actor throwing a drink in a rival's face. "Enough!" you declare as if your devices will applaud your newfound resolve. Then there are the over-the-top relaxation techniques that follow—perhaps a bubble bath worthy of a movie montage, complete with cucumbers over your eyes and an Enya playlist. Despite its theatrics, it's a scene that underscores a crucial truth: we desperately need time away from screens to recharge our minds and bodies.

So, how do we rejuvenate our weary minds amidst the relentless demands of the digital world? One simple yet effective strategy is the 20-20-20 rule: for every 20 minutes spent staring at a screen, look at something 20 feet away for 20 seconds. It's a small act of rebellion against screen fatigue, a chance for your eyes to relax and reset. Imagine it as a mini-vacation for your eyeballs, a momentary escape from the tyranny of pixels. But mental rejuvenation requires more than just eye breaks. Engaging in outdoor activities can be a powerful antidote to tech-induced stress. Whether it's a leisurely walk in the park, a jog around the block, or a game of fetch with your dog, stepping outside provides a much-needed breath of fresh air. Nature has a way of soothing our frazzled nerves, offering a change of scenery that helps us disconnect from digital chaos and reconnect with the world around us.

Creating a balanced tech-life routine is crucial for maintaining mental well-being. Start by scheduling regular tech breaks throughout your day. Treat these breaks with the importance they deserve, like any other task on your calendar. Set an alarm if you must, but make sure to honor these moments of respite. Incorporating mindfulness or meditation practices can also be transformative. Consider dedicating a few minutes each day to simply breathe and be present. These moments of stillness can act as an anchor amidst the storm of notifications and updates, allowing you to center yourself and find calm. Designing an evening routine that promotes restful sleep is another essential piece of the puzzle. Create a pre-bedtime ritual that signals to your brain it's time to wind down. This might involve dimming the lights, sipping herbal tea, or curling up with a good book—one made of actual paper, not pixels.

In closing this chapter, we've explored the impact of screen fatigue on our mental and physical health, the humor in our quirky attempts to escape it, and practical strategies for finding balance. As we move forward, let's remember that while technology is an integral part of our lives, it doesn't have to dominate them. Embracing these practices can help us create a healthier relationship with our screens, allowing us to thrive in a world that often feels like it's moving at the speed of light. Next, we'll delve into the complexities of digital relationships, exploring how to nurture genuine connections in an increasingly connected world.

# TWELVE

# Satirical Glossary of Tech Terms

I f you've ever felt like you're trying to decode a secret language when scrolling through social media, you're not alone. The digital world brims with a lexicon that's as dynamic as it is perplexing. It's a place where "authentic content" may not be as genuine as it sounds, and "flame wars" rage with all the ferocity of a dragon defending its lair. Let's dive into this linguistic jungle and uncover the humor tucked between the hashtags.

The term "authentic content" gets thrown around a lot in influencer circles, often used to describe a supposedly unfiltered and raw post. But let's be honest: when an influencer touts their latest "no-filter" snap, there's a good chance it was shot with the strategic lighting of a Hollywood set. In these cases, authenticity becomes a performance, a carefully curated version of reality that's as raw as a perfectly staged food photo. Then there's "collab," a buzzword that suggests a mutual convergence of creative energies. In truth, it's often more of a marketing ploy, a handshake sealed with a wink and a nod that says, "I'll scratch your back if you scratch mine." It's less about genuine enthusiasm and more about doubling the reach of sponsored content. "Engagement," another favorite, is less about meaningful interaction and more about tallying the number of strangers who grace your post with heart emojis. It's a number game where actual human connection is the uninvited guest at the party.

On the darker side of our digital dictionary lies the language of trolls. These are the internet's mischief-makers, the digital equivalent of the neighborhood kid who rings your doorbell and runs away. "Flame war" describes the escalating chaos of an online argument where rationality is the first casualty, and participants hurl insults like confetti at a particularly dysfunctional parade. It's a spectacle that can be both entertaining and exhausting, leaving you wondering why you ventured into the comments section in the first place. "Baiting" is the troll's favorite pastime, where they post controversial opinions like fishing lines, hoping to reel in unsuspecting responders. It's a dance of provocation and reaction, a game where the only prize is the sweet satisfaction of chaos unleashed.

The evolution of digital language is nothing short of fascinating and sometimes hilarious. The role of an "influencer" has become a legitimate career that might leave you chuckling if you remember when the term first emerged. The job title blends personal branding with social media savvy, turning everyday tasks into content opportunities. Meanwhile, trolling has morphed from a fishing technique into an art form of online mischief, a shift that speaks volumes about our digital age. As trolls have become cultural icons, they've helped shape the chaotic humor that defines much internet interaction today.

In this ever-changing landscape, new-age digital terminology continues to sprout like weeds in a neglected garden. Consider "like-spamming," the practice of inundating someone's feed with likes to grab their attention. It's the digital equivalent of a toddler tugging at your sleeve, insistent and relentless. Or "emoji-lution," which refers to the gradual replacement of words with emojis in digital communication. This evolution has turned our messages into modern hieroglyphs, where a string of tiny faces can convey more than a paragraph ever could. It's a testament to our creativity and desire for brevity, a nod to how language adapts to the digital age.

### *Case Study: Rethinking Digital Lingo*

Emma, a marketing consultant, noticed that her vocabulary was filled with digital buzzwords she often used without a second thought. Words like "pivot," "optimize," and "viral" had become part of her daily language, especially in client meetings. One day, while chatting with a friend who worked outside the tech world, Emma realized how many of these phrases sounded like jargon. Her friend joked about the "language of digital natives," Emma began wondering if she was speaking in buzzwords more than in actual meaning. Curious, she made a list of terms she used regularly, writing down humorous or satirical definitions for each.

As she shared this list with colleagues and friends, they all laughed at the creative definitions, realizing how detached some of these terms had become from their original meanings. Inspired by the exercise, Emma began using more straightforward language in her conversations, especially with clients. By reflecting on her "digital speak," she gained a fresh perspective on how she communicated and found that simplifying her language made her conversations clearer and more relatable. The exercise reminded her of the playful side of digital language and helped her connect more genuinely with others.

**Lesson**: Emma's experience highlights the value of examining and simplifying our digital vocabulary. By understanding the true meanings behind the buzzwords, she communicated more effectively and brought humor into her language, making her conversations feel more authentic and engaging.

### *Interactive Exercise: Decoding Your Digital Speak*

Take a moment to reflect on your own digital vocabulary. Are there terms you use without considering their true meaning? Consider compiling a list of buzzwords and their satirical definitions to share with friends. You might find humor in examining how your language has evolved and even invent a few terms of your own. This exercise sharpens your linguistic awareness and lets you appreciate the playful nature of digital communication.

As we navigate this world of quirky terms and hidden meanings, remember that language is as much about connection as it is about understanding. Whether you're decoding influencer lingo or sidestepping trolls, the words we choose shape our digital identities and interactions. Every term in this colorful, ever-evolving dictionary of digital life tells a story—often more humorous than you might expect.

## The Algorithm Ate My Homework: A Glossary of Excuses

In true human fashion, technology has handed us a whole new set of excuses—each one more clever (and hilarious) than the last! Consider the ever-popular "The Cloud Ate It." This excuse is a modern twist on the classic "dog ate my homework," where we attribute data loss to the mysterious and often misunderstood cloud. The cloud, in reality, is nothing more than a network of servers, but it has taken on an almost mythical status. It's the perfect scapegoat for when you've misplaced a crucial file or accidentally deleted that presentation for Monday's meeting. "I Was Hacked" is another classic, often dusted off when someone posts an embarrassing status or a questionable photo. It offers a convenient escape hatch, suggesting that some nefarious entity is behind your digital missteps rather than admitting you might have had one too many glasses of wine while scrolling through social media.

These excuses aren't just about shifting blame; they're mini-dramas, each with its own narrative flair. Picture this: your Wi-Fi goes down in the middle of a crucial deadline, and you find yourself frantically typing, "Sorry, Wi-Fi woes!" It's a phrase that conjures images of tangled cables and blinking modems, a plea for understanding in a world that runs on connectivity. Then there's the infamous "Zoom Freeze," a term that's become all too familiar in the age of remote work. We've all been there—mid-sentence, making a crucial point when suddenly your face contorts and freezes on screen. A moment suspended in time becomes the perfect excuse for missing part of the meeting, leaving you to sheepishly explain your digital disappearance once you reconnect.

But why stop at the classics when we can invent new excuses for our tech mishaps? Enter "Algorithmic Amnesia," a convenient way to explain forgetting an appointment or deadline because the algorithm didn't remind you. It's as if we've outsourced our memory to the digital gods, and when they fail us, we claim amnesia. Or consider "Buffering Brain," where you liken your blanking out during a conversation to a video that keeps buffering. Just as the spinning wheel of death taunts us on slow internet connections, our minds sometimes need a moment to catch up, and this excuse provides a humorous way to admit it.

There's a fascinating psychology behind why we lean on technology as a crutch for our oversights. Blaming tech jargon allows us to sidestep accountability with a dash of humor and tech-savvy flair. It's far easier to say, "The cloud ate my report," than to admit you forgot to save your work. Technology offers a built-in scapegoat, a comforting buffer between us and our own human errors. It's like having an imaginary friend to take the fall when things go awry. In a world where we're constantly juggling digital demands, these excuses serve as tiny lifeboats we cling to when the digital tide threatens to pull us under.

Our desire to connect in a disconnected world is at the heart of these excuses. They're a way to find common ground and laugh over the absurdity of our tech-dependent lives. Whether it's the cloud's appetite or a buffering brain, these excuses remind us that behind every screen is a human trying to navigate the chaos. So the next time technology lets you down, embrace the humor in the situation, craft your own excuse, and share a knowing nod with those who've been there, too.

## Swipe Left on This: Comical Tech Terms Defined

Navigating dating apps can feel like entering a world where communication has its own unique rhythm and language. Take "catfishing," for instance, which involves pretending to be someone else online to reel in unsuspecting matches. It's a digital masquerade, where the mask isn't just a misleading profile picture but an entirely fabricated identity. The term gained notoriety as people discovered that their charming online suitors were actually more fiction than fact. Then there's "ghosting," a term that perfectly encapsulates the eerie experience of someone disappearing from your digital life without a trace. One minute, you're exchanging witty banter; the next, your messages are filled with a haunting silence. Both terms highlight the peculiar ways we navigate relationships in an online space where anonymity can be both a shield and a sword.

Of course, dating apps come with their own brand of exhaustion, aptly named "swipe fatigue." It's the weariness that sets in after endless swiping sessions in search of a match that doesn't turn into a digital pumpkin by morning. This fatigue is a reminder that sometimes, searching for connection can feel more like a chore than a choice. Then there's "profile peacocking," where users over-exaggerate their qualities in bios that read like a mix between a resume and a reality TV audition. These profiles promise adventurous spirits and world-class chefs but often deliver little more than couch potatoes with a penchant for takeout. It's a game of show and tell, where the stakes are as high as the creativity of the claims being made.

As the digital landscape evolves, so does the language we use to describe our experiences. Enter "scrolliosis," a play on the physical ailment that humorously describes the back pain we develop from too much scrolling. It's a testament to our screen-bound habits, where hours can slip by in the blink of an eye, and the only evidence of our digital adventures is the crick in our neck. And then there's "appathy," a clever term for the apathy we feel toward the overwhelming number of apps clamoring for our attention. It captures the fatigue of sifting through a sea of icons, each promising to improve our lives but often only adding to the clutter.

Tech slang doesn't just reflect our current culture; it helps shape it. The global reach of terms like "meme" and "viral" shows how language evolves and spreads across borders, creating a shared understanding that transcends geography. These terms have become part of our everyday vocabulary, influencing how we communicate online and offline. The impact is so profound that it prompts us to rethink traditional language norms, integrating tech slang into our daily dialogues in subtle and significant ways. According to a study on the impact of social media on language evolution, these changes reflect the democratization of language, where diverse users influence linguistic trends and create micro-languages within online communities. This evolution is not just about words; it's about connecting, engaging, and sharing in a world where communication has no bounds.

As we wrap up this exploration of digital vocabulary, it's clear that our tech terms are more than just words. They're reflections of our social interactions, the quirks of modern life, and the humor we find in navigating it all. This glossary of the absurd is a reminder that language is as dynamic as the culture it represents, always growing, adapting, and, most importantly, keeping us laughing through it all. So, the next time you find yourself lost in the sea of swipes, scrolls, and digital dialogues, take a moment to appreciate the colorful language that captures the essence of our online experiences.

# THIRTEEN

# The Future of Digital Culture

In a world where my smart refrigerator seems to have a higher IQ than some people I know, it's time to ponder the future of digital culture. Imagine a realm where AI-driven cities hum along like well-oiled machines, promising a utopian existence where crime rates plummet to zero thanks to vigilant algorithms. Your morning commute could be a breezy affair, with AI predicting and preventing traffic jams before you even finish your protein shake. In this ideal world, universal basic income would be generously funded by tech giants, allowing you to focus on your passions—like finally mastering the art of sourdough or binge-watching every docuseries known to humanity. Education, too, would undergo a radical transformation, with personalized learning experiences delivered through virtual reality classrooms, where every student gets the individual attention they deserve, even if it means the AI occasionally glitches and calls you "Steve" instead of "Sarah."

But before we get too comfortable in this digital paradise, let's consider the flipside, where technology plays Dr. Jekyll and Mr. Hyde. Picture this: a dystopian nightmare where surveillance states run rampant, scrutinizing your every move under the guise of safety. In this grim reality, algorithms dictate your social status through "Happiness Metrics," determining whether you're worthy of that promotion or if you'll be relegated to a life of mediocrity. The digital class system becomes the new norm, with social media influence serving as currency, while those less inclined to post selfies become the "have-nots" in a society obsessed with likes and shares. As automation takes over, the workforce dwindles, and human jobs become a relic of the past, leaving us to wonder if our sole purpose is to provide Wi-Fi for our new robot overlords.

Of course, we can't discuss the future without poking fun at its more outlandish possibilities. Imagine a world where your vacation is spent entirely in a virtual paradise, complete with sandy beaches and tropical drinks, all from the comfort of your couch. Who needs sunscreen when your biggest worry is your cat walking across the VR headset? The absurdity of these extremes highlights the need to balance our digital dreams with a healthy dose of realism. After all, it's the quirks and imperfections of the human experience that make life truly interesting.

So, how do we navigate this brave new world without losing our humanity? Start by considering the ethical implications of technological advancements, a less glamorous but crucial aspect of innovation. Ensuring that technology serves us, rather than vice versa, means prioritizing transparency, accountability, and inclusivity in development. Protecting human agency in an increasingly automated landscape requires vigilance. It's about creating a digital future that enriches our lives instead of dictating them. As we stand on the brink of this digital evolution, it's essential to approach it with curiosity and caution, blending optimism with a grounding sense of reality.

### *Case Study: Imagining a Balanced Digital Future*

Carlos, a high school teacher and self-described "tech enthusiast," found himself both excited and cautious about emerging technologies. He loved using virtual reality for immersive learning experiences in his classroom but felt uneasy about AI's potential to replace personal interactions. Inspired by a reflection exercise, Carlos decided to map out his ideal digital future, listing technologies he looked forward to and those that raised concerns. He imagined a future where tech could enhance learning and bring people together without overshadowing the human connections he valued deeply.

After putting his thoughts to paper, Carlos shared his vision with his family and friends, sparking a lively conversation about tech's role in their lives. They discussed everything from the thrill of self-driving cars to worries about data privacy, finding common ground in their desire for a future that balanced innovation with authenticity. This exercise helped Carlos clarify his priorities and reaffirm his commitment to using technology in ways that aligned with his values. By envisioning his ideal digital future, Carlos found a path forward where he could embrace tech's potential without losing sight of what mattered most.

**Lesson**: Carlos's experience shows the importance of reflecting on our relationship with technology as we shape our digital futures. By balancing excitement with caution and sharing his vision with others, he found clarity on navigating the digital world in a way that aligns with his values and priorities.

### *Interactive Exercise: Envisioning Your Digital Future*

Take a moment to imagine your ideal digital future. What technologies excite you? Which ones concern you? Reflect on how you can balance embracing innovation with maintaining the values that matter most to you. Write down your thoughts, and consider sharing them with friends or family to spark a conversation about the future we're collectively shaping.

As we chart our course through the future of digital culture, let's remember that the power to shape this landscape lies within each of us. With a blend of humor, practicality, and a touch of skepticism, we can confidently navigate the digital frontier, ensuring that it enhances our lives rather than overwhelms them.

## The Rise of the Machines: Tech's Next Frontier

Imagine a future where machines assist and understand us—where humanoid robots walk among us with personalities as distinct as your best friend's. These machines would not just respond to commands but engage in conversations, empathize with your mood swings, and maybe even offer a shoulder to cry on—though, hopefully, not a literal one made of cold steel. The potential for machines to gain sentience and autonomy is no longer just the stuff of science fiction. Picture AI companions tailored to individual preferences, learning your quirks and habits to become the ultimate personal assistant. They could suggest your favorite playlist before you even think to ask or remind you to drink water because, let's be honest, we could all use a little hydration nudge. But let's not forget, these AI pals might also develop a penchant for sarcasm, tossing in a sly comment about your questionable attire choices before a video call.

Integrating machines into our everyday lives promises humor and a few eyebrow-raising moments. Imagine robotic pets replacing traditional animals, offering companionship without the fur. A robotic dog that doesn't shed or require walks might sound ideal until it starts heckling you for your lack of exercise. And then there are AI assistants whose personalities are dialed up to eleven, complete with over-the-top enthusiasm. You might find yourself in the kitchen, preparing breakfast while your AI assistant chimes in with unsolicited cooking tips, offering everything from the perfect pancake flip to a full-blown motivational speech about the virtues of a balanced breakfast.

Yet, as we inch closer to this future, we must confront the challenges of granting machines more autonomy. Decision-making dilemmas arise in scenarios like AI-driven vehicles, where split-second choices between two unfavorable outcomes could mean the difference between a fender bender and a more serious accident. These machines, lacking in human intuition and morality, may need help navigating real-world situations' complexities. There's also the potential for AI to challenge human authority, question our decisions or even make autonomous choices that differ from our expectations. Imagine your AI assistant deciding that today is the day you finally try skydiving, based on an algorithm it cooked up after analyzing your recent search history.

As we contemplate these challenges, we also look forward to innovations that could redefine our relationship with machines. Brain-computer interfaces may soon enhance our cognition, allowing us to interact with technology using just our thoughts. Advanced robotics in healthcare could revolutionize elderly care, providing assistance and companionship to those in need. These robots might remind you to take your medication or entertain you with a story, all while knitting you a sweater—though, given their mechanical nature, the sweater might look more like a modern art installation.

The rise of machines invites us to explore new possibilities while maintaining a healthy dose of skepticism and humor. After all, as technology evolves, so must our approach to living alongside it. Balancing innovation with practicality ensures that our digital companions add value to our lives without overshadowing the essence of what makes us human.

## Digital Culture: Navigating Tomorrow's Trends

In the whirlwind of digital evolution, emerging trends are reshaping our cultural landscape with a flair that's equally fascinating and bewildering. Take virtual influencers, for instance. Imagine following an influencer who never has a bad hair day, never tires, and never posts an unflattering angle. These AI-generated personas are becoming the new faces of brand campaigns, effortlessly bridging the gap between fiction and reality. They're not just CGI characters; they're digital celebrities with their own backstories and personalities, living lives that might make even the most polished human influencers green with envy. As they gain popularity, you might find yourself questioning whether your favorite fashion tips come from a real person or a pixelated enigma.

Meanwhile, social media is undergoing a transformation of its own, morphing into immersive virtual worlds that would make the creators of "The Matrix" nod in approval. Platforms are evolving into spaces where you're not just scrolling through feeds but walking through digital landscapes, attending virtual concerts, or having face-to-face chats with your friends' avatars. This evolution promises a level of interaction that's as exciting as it is daunting, offering new ways to connect while blurring the lines between the digital and physical realms. Imagine meeting someone for the first time, not in a coffee shop but in a beautifully rendered virtual café, complete with digital lattes and virtual pastries that are somehow calorie-free.

As we adapt to these trends, humor becomes an invaluable ally, lightening the load of what might otherwise feel like a steep learning curve. Picture the chaos of using augmented reality in everyday tasks, like navigating your kitchen with AR goggles that insist on labeling every item, from your toaster to your cat. Or the comedic potential of virtual reality mishaps, where you find yourself swinging wildly at invisible foes, much to the amusement of anyone watching in the real world. The ability to laugh at these moments and embrace the absurdity of new technology can turn what might be a source of stress into a delightful adventure.

These trends also have profound implications for human interaction, reshaping how we connect with each other and with technology. As digital and physical identities blend, the line between online personas and real-world selves becomes increasingly porous. You might curate your virtual avatar to reflect the best version of yourself, but balancing authenticity with digital expression becomes a nuanced dance. Meanwhile, new forms of digital etiquette emerge as we learn to navigate social norms in spaces where a virtual wave replaces a handshake, and the phrase "ghosting" takes on a whole new meaning. It's a brave new world where manners are redefined, and the rules are written as we go.

Staying informed and adaptable is key to preparing for this digital evolution. Engage with tech communities and thought leaders who are at the forefront of these changes, offering insights and predictions. Whether through online forums, podcasts, or social media, staying connected to these conversations can help you understand and anticipate the shifts in digital culture. Continuous learning and skill development in digital literacy are equally important, ensuring you're not just a passive observer but an active participant in this ever-changing landscape.

As we wrap up our exploration of tomorrow's trends, remember that the future is both thrilling and unpredictable. It's a dance of innovation where humor and adaptability will serve you well. In this digital age, the only constant is change, and the best way to navigate it is with open eyes, an open mind, and a smile. Now, as we look ahead to the next chapter, let's consider how we can create a digital life that's worth living and enriches and empowers us.

# FOURTEEN

# Creating a Digital Life Worth Living

Imagine scrolling through your social media feed and feeling an odd sense of déjà vu, like every post is a version of the last. You realize you've been caught in the loop of digital monotony, where your online identity feels as curated as a museum exhibit, each piece carefully selected to project an image of perfection. But here's a thought—what if you could craft a digital narrative that genuinely reflects who you are, imperfections and all? This chapter is about breaking free from the pressure to filter reality, embracing authenticity, and realizing that your online presence can be as unique as you are.

Defining your digital identity begins with choosing content that aligns with your personal values. It's about sharing stories and experiences that resonate with you, not just the ones that earn the most likes. Crafting a consistent and honest digital persona can be both liberating and challenging. It's easy to succumb to the temptation of projecting a picture-perfect life but doing so often leads to a disconnect between your online self and reality. Embrace the quirks, the unfiltered moments, and the genuine connections.

Your digital narrative should reflect your true self, not a facade built to impress others.

The humor in narrative creation lies in the absurdity of maintaining a flawless online image. We've all experienced the struggle of balancing authenticity with privacy, like when you're torn between posting a candid photo or editing it to perfection. It's the digital equivalent of deciding whether to wear your favorite pajamas to a formal event. While privacy is important, it's equally crucial to remember that perfection is an illusion. Embrace the imperfections and laugh at the moments that didn't go as planned. These stories resonate with others and make your digital presence relatable and genuine.

To build your digital narrative, leverage digital tools and platforms that support authenticity. Blogging platforms offer a space to share your personal stories. At the same time, social media tools help curate and schedule content, allowing you to maintain a coherent online persona without succumbing to the pressure of constant posting. These tools can be your allies, helping you share content that aligns with your values and fostering connections that matter. With the right approach, your digital identity can become a source of empowerment, not stress.

### Case Study: Aligning the Digital Self with the Real Self

An aspiring writer, Rachel spent a lot of time curating her online presence to look polished and professional. She carefully selected photos, wrote thoughtful captions, and posted regular project updates. However, she started feeling a disconnect between her online image and her real-life experiences. While her social media showed a confident, successful writer, Rachel often felt uncertain about her work and rarely shared her struggles. Curious about how others perceived her online, she asked a few close friends for honest feedback on her digital persona. Their responses surprised her—they admired her posts but felt her online presence was "a bit too perfect" and less relatable than the Rachel they knew.

Encouraged by their feedback, Rachel decided to bring more authenticity to her online narrative. She started sharing candid moments, discussing the ups and downs of her creative process, and showing her audience the behind-the-scenes reality of her life as a writer. To her surprise, her posts received positive responses, connecting people to her honesty and vulnerability. The experience helped Rachel bridge the gap between her online persona and her true self, building a more genuine connection with her followers and boosting her self-confidence.

**Lesson**: Rachel's story highlights the importance of aligning our digital and real-life identities. By seeking honest feedback and embracing authenticity, she created a digital narrative that genuinely reflected who she was, fostering more meaningful connections online.

### *Interactive Exercise: Evaluating and Seeking Feedback*

Take a moment to evaluate your online interactions and their effects on your self-esteem. Reflect on the content you share and how it influences your personal life and community. Consider seeking feedback from trusted peers about your online persona. Are you portraying the person you truly are, or is there a disconnect between your digital and real-life selves? Use this feedback to refine your digital narrative, ensuring it accurately represents who you are and what you stand for. Remember, the most powerful digital identities reflect authenticity and inspire connection.

## The Life Algorithm: Designing a Happier Online Experience

Imagine your digital life as a carefully curated garden, where algorithms act as mischievous gardeners. They decide which plants (or content) get the most sunlight, often surprising you with their choices. Algorithms shape our online experiences, tailoring content to keep us engaged. They learn from our clicks, likes, and even the things we scroll past. It's like having a personal DJ who occasionally sneaks in a track you never requested. To turn this to your advantage, start personalizing your content feeds. Follow creators and join communities that resonate with your interests and values. This enhances your online experience and shields you from the algorithmic whims that might otherwise lead you down an endless rabbit hole of cat videos.

Now, let's talk about the quirks of living in an algorithm-driven world. Have you ever wondered why your recommendation engine seems convinced you're obsessed with medieval cooking techniques or underwater basket weaving? The comedy of algorithmic assumptions can be baffling and entertaining. It's as if these digital matchmakers have a sense of humor, suggesting content that makes you question your browsing history. Embrace these moments with a chuckle, but also remain vigilant. Recognize when algorithms steer you toward extremes or content that doesn't align with your true self. Resisting these manipulations is key to maintaining a balanced digital presence.

Balancing algorithmic suggestions with human judgment is vital to creating a positive digital ecosystem. While algorithms can introduce us to new interests, they shouldn't dictate our entire online experience. Curate your content manually, supplementing algorithmic recommendations with your own discoveries. Think of it as blending the best of both worlds—human intuition and machine efficiency. Use critical thinking to evaluate the relevance of suggested content. This approach empowers you to be the architect of your digital environment, ensuring it supports your well-being and personal growth. Let's build an online world that reflects our values and aspirations, one where we navigate with purpose and joy.

## Digital Zen: Finding Peace in the Tech Storm

Picture this: you're sitting in your living room, attempting to meditate with the help of a mindfulness app, while your phone buzzes with notifications like a hyperactive bee. The irony isn't lost on you—using technology to escape technology can feel like trying to extinguish a fire with a flamethrower. Yet, achieving digital zen is possible with a few mindful practices. Start by incorporating meditation and mindfulness apps into your daily routine. Despite their digital nature, these tools offer guided sessions that anchor you amidst the chaos. Consider establishing tech-free zones at home or work. Designate areas where devices are persona non grata, helping you carve out moments of uninterrupted tranquility.

Finding humor in the quest for digital peace can lighten the load. Imagine the scene: you're deep in meditation when a notification alert jars you back to reality, like a zen monk startled by a whoopee cushion. It's a comedic reminder that achieving calm in a connected world isn't always seamless. Embrace these moments with a chuckle. Practical techniques can help maintain tranquility. Practice deep breathing exercises during tech breaks, using each breath as a reset button. Set visual reminders to pause and breathe—sticky notes on your laptop or a calming screensaver can work wonders.

Creating a tranquil digital space is more than aesthetics; it's about curating an environment that promotes relaxation and focus. Use calming wallpapers and screensavers that soothe rather than stimulate. Organize apps and files to reduce clutter, like a digital version of Marie Kondo tidying your desktop. A well-organized digital space fosters a sense of calm, allowing you to engage with technology on your own terms.

## The Digital Balance Challenge: Humor Meets Habit

Picture this: you're trying to unwind after a long day, phone in hand, mindlessly scrolling. Suddenly, you realize it's well past midnight, and you've sneakily watched eight cat videos, read three conspiracy theories, and somehow landed on an article about the cultural significance of llamas. In today's tech-saturated world, finding balance isn't just about unplugging for set hours; it's about creating boundaries where screen time doesn't overshadow real life. Imagine striking a harmony between your virtual existence and the tangible world, where work emails don't tailgate your dinner, and social media doesn't crash your weekends. Easier said than done, right? It's a tightrope walk over a sea of digital distractions, yet it's crucial for our well-being.

Balancing digital life comes with its own set of hilarious challenges. Have you ever tried to put your phone down before bed, only to find yourself trapped in an endless loop of "just one more" scroll? Or attempted the Olympic feat of cooking dinner while texting, posting, and watching a tutorial on pasta-making—all at once? The modern multitasker could give a circus juggler a run for their money. But fear not; there are ways to sway the balance in your favor. Start by crafting a digital schedule that champions offline activities. Use apps designed to track and limit screen time, giving you a gentle nudge to reconnect with the world beyond the pixels.

Incorporating balance into your life isn't about drastic changes; it's about subtle shifts. Set tech-free times for meals and gatherings, like stacking phones in a "digital detox bowl" before dinner, ensuring conversations remain face-to-face. Dive into hobbies that don't involve screens—maybe dust off that old guitar or finally try your hand at painting. These activities not only break the digital spell but also enrich your day with creativity and connection. Balancing your digital life is less about abstinence and more about moderation, making room for the moments that make life truly vibrant.

## Unplugged and Thriving: Living Beyond the Screen

Imagine the world without the constant hum of notifications—where face-to-face interactions deepen relationships and creativity flows freely without digital noise. Unplugging offers mental and physical rewards that are both profound and refreshing. You open yourself to real conversations and genuine connections when you step away from the screen. The absence of digital distractions allows focus to sharpen, enabling you to engage in activities that truly matter. Creativity finds room to breathe, and ideas once stifled by constant connectivity begin to flourish. It's a reminder that sometimes, disconnecting is the best way to recharge.

The initial awkwardness of unplugging can be comical in its own right. Picture this: you've turned off your devices, and suddenly, you find yourself with more free time than you know what to do with. It's like discovering a hidden room in your house you never knew existed. The first instinct might be to fill this newfound space with activity—perhaps trying your hand at knitting or attempting to bake bread from scratch, only to realize you've created a doughy disaster. But here's the beauty of it: these moments of trial and error, filled with laughter and unexpected joy, make unplugging so liberating.

Consider planning offline adventures as a way to explore life beyond digital interactions. Step into nature, where the rustle of leaves and birds chirping replace the constant ping of notifications. Whether it's a hike in the mountains, a bike ride through the countryside, or a simple walk in the park, these experiences ground you in the present. Local events and community gatherings offer meaningful opportunities to connect with others, fostering a sense of belonging and shared experience. These moments remind us of the richness of life that exists away from screens.

Reflecting on unplugging experiences can offer valuable insights into the impact on your well-being. Consider journaling about the feelings and realizations that emerge during these tech-free periods. What have you discovered about yourself, your relationships, or your priorities? Sharing these stories with friends and family enriches your understanding and encourages others to embrace the benefits of unplugging. It's a chance to celebrate the moments of clarity and connection that arise when you step away from the digital world.

## The Social Media Sabbatical: Embracing Absence

Imagine waking up one morning, and instead of reaching for your phone to scroll through the latest memes, you take a deep breath and enjoy the stillness. Welcome to the concept of a social media sabbatical, a delightful pause from the endless cycle of notifications and updates. Constant social media use can be as exhausting as running a marathon on a treadmill—lots of effort, but you're not really getting anywhere. The relentless barrage of posts and tweets often leaves us feeling more drained than connected. Taking a step back offers a chance to recharge and reflect, like hitting the reset button on your mental health. In these quiet moments, you gain perspective, realizing how much time you spent online and how little it truly impacted your life.

Embarking on this sabbatical can lead to unexpected discoveries. You might be bewildered at how much of your day was previously spent glued to a screen. Without the familiar glow of your phone, you might feel an amusing void, like a detective without a mystery to solve. Some fill this gap with hobbies they never had time for, while others rediscover forgotten passions. It's like discovering a trail in the woods you always sensed was there but never chose to follow. The humorous part comes when you try to fill this newfound time and end up attempting activities like cross-stitching or interpretive dance —things you'd never considered before.

Planning a successful sabbatical involves setting clear goals and timeframes. Decide how long you'll be off the grid and what you hope to achieve. Inform friends and followers to prevent any digital search parties. Reflecting on the insights gained during this break is crucial. Note changes in mood and productivity and identify new interests that emerged. Maybe you'll find that without the constant stream of updates, you have more time for that book you always meant to read or the project you kept postponing. As you step away from the digital noise, you might discover that life offline is richer, more vibrant, and full of possibilities.

## Becoming a Digital Minimalist: Less is More

Imagine your digital life as a cluttered attic filled with forgotten trinkets and outdated gadgets. Digital minimalism invites you to clear the cobwebs, focusing only on what truly matters. Reducing digital clutter enhances mental clarity and productivity, allowing you to prioritize meaningful interactions over mindless scrolling. It's like Marie Kondo for your tech life—if a file, app, or account doesn't spark joy or serve a purpose, it's time to let it go. Picture the satisfaction of a decluttered home screen, free from the tyranny of notification badges and endless app folders.

Embracing digital minimalism isn't without its challenges. The irony of needing an app to help declutter other apps is not lost on us. It's a bit like hiring a personal trainer to help you stop eating cake, only to end up discussing the latest recipes. Yet, humor can ease the transition. Imagine the exaggerated decluttering sessions where you download a minimalist app only to realize it's one more thing to manage. The rewards, however, are well worth the effort as you find yourself navigating a cleaner, more intentional digital space.

Practical steps to minimalism involve organizing digital files and apps, much like tidying a physical workspace. Create folders for essential documents and delete redundant apps that serve no real purpose. Limiting active social media accounts can streamline your online interactions, reducing the noise and allowing for more genuine connections. Sustaining these habits requires regular reviews of your digital belongings and setting intentional goals for your online engagement. By fostering a minimalist digital lifestyle, you reclaim time and focus and create space for what truly matters in your life.

## The Humor of Tech Failures: Lessons in Resilience

There's something undeniably hilarious about a tech failure. Picture this: you're working on a crucial project, feeling like a modern-day Da Vinci, when suddenly, your software crashes with an error message that might as well be hieroglyphics. You stare at the screen, blinking in disbelief, before bursting into laughter at the absurdity of it all. These moments, while frustrating, offer a unique opportunity to find humor in chaos. Tech support interactions can feel like a sitcom, with you as the hapless protagonist trying to explain your woes to a voice that seems to exist in a parallel universe. Laughing at these glitches not only lightens the mood but also fosters resilience.

Resilience thrives in the face of digital setbacks. Learning to adapt to new technologies and embrace mistakes is key. It's about developing a growth mindset, where each failure is a stepping stone, not a stumbling block. Remember the exaggerated drama when you lose unsaved work? That sinking feeling followed by the frantic search for backups? These experiences, while exasperating, teach us the importance of saving often and staying calm under pressure. Humor plays a role here, too. Trying unconventional methods to fix tech issues might involve turning the device off and on again or giving it a gentle tap, hoping it miraculously revives. These attempts remind us to stay light-hearted, even when things go awry. Documenting lessons from each failure and sharing stories of resilience can be a source of mutual encouragement, turning setbacks into a shared learning experience.

## A New Digital Dawn: Your Path Forward in a Tech World

Imagine a future where technology feels more like a helpful assistant than an overbearing boss. It's within reach if we prioritize advancements that genuinely enhance our lives, not just add to the noise. Imagine a world where digital tools align with your personal values, helping you forge meaningful interactions instead of drowning you in notifications. Consider what matters to you, and let those priorities guide your tech usage. Whether connecting more deeply with loved ones or pursuing creative passions, technology should be a means, not an end.

Humor, as always, can be a useful tool when thinking about the future. Predicting tech trends is like trying to forecast the weather on Mars. Will we all have robotic houseplants? Perhaps. The irony of planning in such an unpredictable landscape is that reality often has its own ideas. But that's part of the fun. Embrace the uncertainty with a smile, and let it fuel your creativity. Craft a personal tech vision by setting goals that reflect your aspirations. Whether learning a new skill or building a digital portfolio, align your choices with where you want to go.

Adaptability is crucial in this ever-changing digital world. Stay informed about emerging technologies, and be ready to learn and grow. Lifelong learning isn't just a buzzword; it's a survival skill. By embracing change and focusing on growth, you can confidently navigate the future, turning challenges into opportunities and creating a digital life worth living.

# Conclusion

Well, here we are at the end of our journey together through the digital jungle. It's been quite the adventure, hasn't it? We've laughed and cringed, and hopefully, we've learned a thing or two about how to wrestle our digital lives back from the grips of chaos.

Let's take a moment to revisit the core themes we've explored. We've poked fun at our notification-obsessed culture, drawing parallels to Pavlov's dogs in our Pavlovian response to pings and dings. We've explored the privacy paradox, where sharing is caring, but oversharing is often scaring. We've dived into the colorful world of influencers and the often blurry line between reality and the curated lives they portray. And let's not forget our showdown with fake news and clickbait—our valiant effort to navigate the murky waters of misinformation.

But more than just pointing out the absurdities, we've armed ourselves with practical strategies. From customizing notification settings to digital detoxing, we've charted a path to regain control. We've shared a laugh at FOMO, ghosting, and the dopamine frenzy of likes, all while finding ways to break free from these digital traps.

And in the process, hopefully, we've learned to prioritize meaningful connections over mindless scrolling.

Now, here's the part where I encourage you to take the plunge and implement these strategies. Think of it as embarking on a delightful experiment with your digital life at stake. Try setting those boundaries around your screen time and take a social media sabbatical. Who knows what wonders await when we unplug, even if just for a little while? This book isn't just a critique; it's a toolkit for crafting a life where technology serves you, not the other way around.

As we look to the future, let's imagine a world where technology is our ally, not our adversary. A world where AI and digital tools enhance our creativity, productivity, and well-being without overshadowing our humanity. It's a vision where we use humor and empathy to navigate this ever-evolving landscape. In this world, we leverage technology to connect more deeply and not isolate ourselves in echo chambers.

Imagine waking up each day with a sense of digital balance, where your phone is a tool, not a tether. Think of the possibilities of a life where social media is a source of inspiration, not anxiety. This future isn't just a dream; it's a reality within our reach if we choose to be mindful and intentional about how we engage with our screens.

So, dear reader, remember you're not alone in this journey as you close this book. We're all figuring out how to live harmoniously in this tech-driven world. Let's approach it with curiosity, humor, and a dash of skepticism. After all, the quirks and imperfections of our digital experiences are what make them truly memorable.

Thank you for joining me on this exploration of digital life. May the insights and laughter we've shared guide you as you navigate your own digital landscape. Here's to a future where we survive and thrive beyond the social media trap. Keep laughing, keep learning, and keep living a life that's unapologetically your own.

# Help Others Reclaim Their Time – One Review at a Time!

*"The best way to find yourself is to lose yourself in the service of others." – Mahatma Gandhi*

Hey there! Since you've made it through *Unfriend the Algorithm*, you're now in the "tech-sanity" club. We've tackled social media spirals and notification overload and learned how to reclaim control with a bit of humor along the way. I'm so glad you joined me on this journey to a healthier digital life, and I hope you got a laugh or two and some new perspectives.

Now, I have a small favor to ask. Imagine someone else—maybe a little too glued to their screen, unsure where to start—stumbling upon this book, wondering if it might help them, too. Like you, they're ready to take control but need that little nudge to dive in.

Would you help them out by sharing your honest opinion? Your review could be the push they need to join the mission, take back their time, and unplug a bit.

Your words might make a huge difference. A quick review helps others find what they're looking for and keeps this book visible to others needing it. Whether you loved the laughs, found the tips practical, or enjoyed the break from endless scrolling, your feedback would mean the world to me and the next person ready to unfriend the algorithm.

Share your thoughts and give the next reader a hand.

Scan the QR code to leave your review on Amazon.

Thank you for being part of this journey. Here's to finding more balance, one screen-free moment at a time!

All my best,

Avery Wells

P.S. Every short, long, funny, or serious review helps spread the word and make a difference!

# References


- *Phone Notifications Are Messing With Your Brain* https://www.discovermagazine.com/technology/phone-notifications-are-messing-with-your-brain
- *Prevalence and Pattern of Phantom Ringing and ...* https://www.ncbi.nlm.nih.gov/pmc/articles/PMC6149296/
- *Executives say 'digital detox' retreats are key to their success* https://www.cnn.com/2019/02/07/success/digital-detox-executives/index.html
- *Here's How Social Media Affects Your Mental Health* https://www.mcleanhospital.org/essential/it-or-not-social-medias-affecting-your-mental-health
- *3 Reasons Why You Overshare Online, According To A ...* https://www.forbes.com/sites/traversmark/2023/10/30/3-reasons-why-you-overshare-online-according-to-a-psychologist/
- *7 Real-Life Data Breaches Caused by Insider Threats* https://www.ekransystem.com/en/blog/real-life-examples-insider-threat-caused-breaches
- *What Your Web Browser's Incognito Mode Really Does* https://www.consumerreports.org/electronics-computers/privacy/what-your-web-browsers-incognito-mode-really-does-a8213975018/
- *10 Cringeworthy Social Media Fails of 2017* https://www.krusecontrolinc.com/cringeworthy-social-media-fails-2017/
- *Fear of missing out: A brief overview of origin, theoretical ...* https://www.ncbi.nlm.nih.gov/pmc/articles/PMC8283615/
- *The Effects of Partaking in a Two-Week Social Media ...* https://www.ncbi.nlm.nih.gov/pmc/articles/PMC10740995/
- *The Impact of Social Media on Relationships* https://www.gottman.com/blog/the-impact-of-social-media-on-relationships/
- *28 Witty Responses To Ghosting That'll Haunt Them Forever* https://www.bustle.com/wellness/witty-responses-ghosting
- *The impact of social media influencers on health outcomes* https://www.sciencedirect.com/science/article/pii/S0277953623008298
- *50 Pics That Showcase Instagram Versus Reality In The ...* https://www.boredpanda.com/cringy-insta-vs-reality/
- *Disclosures 101 for Social Media Influencers* https://www.ftc.gov/system/files/documents/plain-language/1001a-influencer-guide-508_1.pdf

- *5 Influencer Marketing Case Studies* https://cdn2.hubspot.net/hubfs/505330/Influencer-Marketing-5-Case-Studies-Ebook.pdf
- *(PDF) Clickbait -Trust and Credibility of Digital News* https://www.researchgate.net/publication/350912220_Clickbait_-Trust_and_Credibility_of_Digital_News
- *FactCheck.org - A Project of The Annenberg Public Policy ...* https://www.factcheck.org/
- *Not Fake News—Satire Is Helping Spread Misinformation ...* https://www.forbes.com/sites/petersuciu/2024/02/02/not-fake-news-satire-is-helping-spread-misinformation-on-social-media/
- *You'll Be Outraged at How Easy It Was to Get You to Click ...* https://www.wired.com/2015/12/psychology-of-clickbait/
- *The Effects of Partaking in a Two-Week Social Media ...* https://www.ncbi.nlm.nih.gov/pmc/articles/PMC10740995/
- *The Infinite Scroll: Why It's So Addictive and How to Break ...* https://freedom.to/blog/infinite-scroll/
- *The surprising power of internet memes* https://www.bbc.com/future/article/20220928-the-surprising-power-of-internet-memes
- *Digital detox: An effective solution in the smartphone era? A ...* https://journals.sagepub.com/doi/full/10.1177/20501579211028647
- *The Cognitive Costs of Multitasking* http://dr-hatfield.com/educ216/Multitasking%20The%20Cognitive%20Costs%20of%20Multitasking.pdf
- *Comparing 'Pomodoro' breaks and self-regulated breaks* https://pubmed.ncbi.nlm.nih.gov/36859717/
- *The effects of smartphone notifications on cognitive control ...* https://www.ncbi.nlm.nih.gov/pmc/articles/PMC9671478/
- *The 10 Best Productivity Apps that use Gamification in 2024* https://yukaichou.com/lifestyle-gamification/the-top-ten-gamified-productivity-apps/
- *50 AI Art Fails That Are Both Horrifying And Hilarious* https://www.boredpanda.com/ai-fails/
- *Algorithmic bias detection and mitigation: Best practices ...* https://www.brookings.edu/articles/algorithmic-bias-detection-and-mitigation-best-practices-and-policies-to-reduce-consumer-harms/
- *Artificial intelligence and its impact on everyday life* https://online.york.ac.uk/artificial-intelligence-and-its-impact-on-everyday-life/
- *Ethical AI: Principles, Best Practices, and Implications* https://rtslabs.com/ensuring-ethical-use-ai-principles-best-practices-implications/
- *The Virtues and Downsides of Online Dating* https://www.pewresearch.org/internet/2020/02/06/the-virtues-and-downsides-of-online-dating/

- *How Social Media Affects Relationships in Modern Times* https://mindbodycounselingreno.com/blog/relationships/how-social-media-affects-relationships/
- *From Online to Offline: How to Transition Digital ...* https://ivyhousecreative.com/blog/from-online-to-offline-how-to-transition-digital-networking-into-real-life-opportunities
- *Make 'Em Laugh: How Humor Can Be the Secret Weapon in ...* https://www.gsb.stanford.edu/insights/make-em-laugh-how-humor-can-be-secret-weapon-your-communication
- *The Mental Health Pitfalls of Wearable Technology* https://www.hitlab.org/mental-health-balance-pitfalls-wearables/
- *Adventures in Self-Surveillance, aka The Quantified ...* https://www.forbes.com/sites/kashmirhill/2011/04/07/adventures-in-self-surveillance-aka-the-quantified-self-aka-extreme-navel-gazing/
- *8 Habit Tracking Apps For Boosting Your Well-Being In 2024* https://www.forbes.com/health/wellness/best-habit-tracking-apps/
- *Why Use Humor as a Motivational Tool in the Workplace?* https://megsoper.com/blog/why-use-humor-as-a-motivational-tool-in-the-workplace/
- *Effects of limiting digital screen use on well-being, mood ...* https://www.nature.com/articles/s44184-022-00015-6
- *The Effects of Partaking in a Two-Week Social Media ...* https://www.ncbi.nlm.nih.gov/pmc/articles/PMC10740995/
- *Stress relief from laughter? It's no joke* https://www.mayoclinic.org/healthy-lifestyle/stress-management/in-depth/stress-relief/art-20044456
- *20-20-20 Rule: Does It Help Prevent Digital Eye Strain?* https://www.healthline.com/health/eye-health/20-20-20-rule
- *Seven Funny-Sounding Tech Terms That Are No Joke* https://www.linkedin.com/pulse/seven-funny-sounding-tech-terms-joke-remie-verougstraete
- *The Impact of Social Media on Language Evolution* https://www.researchgate.net/publication/382186538_The_Impact_of_Social_Media_on_Language_Evolution
- *A brief history of trolls* https://www.dailydot.com/unclick/phillips-brief-history-of-trolls/
- *The indefinable charm of satirical dictionaries | Books* https://www.theguardian.com/books/booksblog/2011/mar/01/satirical-dictionaries
- *Smart Cities Redefined: AI-Driven Urban Planning, ...* https://www.technology-innovators.com/smart-cities-redefined-ai-driven-urban-

planning-infrastructure-optimization-and-citizen-services-in-the-smart-cities/

- *Is It Silicon Valley's Job to Make Guaranteed Income ...* https://www.nytimes.com/2024/07/16/technology/ubi-openai-silicon-valley.html
- *Humanoid Robots Display Realistic Emotions, Thanks to ...* https://www.iotworldtoday.com/robotics/humanoid-robots-display-realistic-emotions-thanks-to-new-research
- *The State of Virtual Influencers in 2024 (Report + Infographic)* https://theinfluencermarketingfactory.com/virtual-influencers-2024/#:~:text=The%20Future%20of%20Virtual%20Influencers,-Virtual%20influencers%20aren
- *Creating Your Personal Brand and Digital Identity* https://jindal.utdallas.edu/blog/creating-your-personal-brand-and-digital-identity/
- *Social media algorithms exploit how we learn from our peers* https://news.northwestern.edu/stories/2023/08/social-media-algorithms-exploit-how-humans-learn-from-their-peers/
- *The benefits of digital minimalism in everyday life* https://techless.com/blogs/resources/the-benefits-of-digital-minimalism-in-everyday-life?srsltid=AfmBOoq4ikFZqP447FLGTpcih3Jil0htrx2cZrdRza ZOASzrjO6Gf2Du
- *Drastic and funny ways of detox against social media* https://onlypult.com/blog/drastic-and-funny-ways-of-detox-against-social-media